TEMPUS
Oral History
SERIES

STAMFORD
voices

The Mid-Lent Fair in Red Lion Square, 1904.

David
Hope you find this interesting.

TEMPUS
Oral History
SERIES

STAMFORD
voices

love

Compiled by
Judith Spelman

Judith
Dec 99

TEMPUS

First published 1999
Copyright © Judith Spelman, 1999

Tempus Publishing Limited
The Mill, Brimscombe Port,
Stroud, Gloucestershire, GL5 2QG

ISBN 0 7524 1603 0

Typesetting and origination by
Tempus Publishing Limited
Printed in Great Britain by
Midway Clark Printing, Wiltshire

To my son, Guy Wyles, who can claim some of his roots in this town

Cover illustration: Some members of the Bowman family
at the turn of the century.

Harry Pond had a reputation as a fine speedskater.

CONTENTS

Foreword   6

Introduction   7

Acknowledgements   8

1. Early Memories   9

2. Schooldays   18

3. Working Life   30

4. Winters   46

5. Leisure and Pleasure   51

6. People and Places   68

7. Markets, Fairs and Festivals   86

8. Shops and Shopkeepers   97

9. Wartime   114

FOREWORD

This book recounts activities and events in the lives of a number of inhabitants of a small market town in Lincolnshire. In common with other professionals, Mrs Spelman has learned to listen rather than cross-question. Thus the individual stories appear utterly genuine. They include the parson's family, professional musicians, tradespeople such as caterers, jewellers, sweet shop dames, engineers, dwellers in slum courts and even the town's eccentrics – there was toleration and room for them in those happier days.

When I came to Stamford in the twenties, the population was under 10,000 – just small enough for each to know the other's business. Of the total, 16 per cent inhabited slum courts as bad as those in Bermondsey and Rotherhithe that I knew as a resident obstetrician at Guy's Hospital. The First World War dealt a mortal blow to the out-of-date customs and privileges of Stamford's social existence but the post-war depression which persisted until 1936, when rearmament began, allowed the old ways to linger on. Agriculture in the surrounding villages absorbed at least six times the present number of skilled land workers in tied cottages, who were preyed upon by tallymen from the adjacent town.

A small army of tramps walked a beat from one workhouse to another (the Public Assistance Acts and the Public Assistance Institutions belong to the early thirties). Gipsies with their caravans abounded and some astonishingly paid their bills in gold half sovereigns. Countrymen bought plovers' eggs, morels and other rare fungi; you could get a good second-hand car for £25 and run it on ROP (Russian) petrol at 1s 6d a gallon! Vintage port – 1904 and 1908 were the current years – cost less than 10s 6d a bottle and was decanted into clean bottles and delivered with the branded cork tied round the bottle neck to prove authenticity by Thomas's wine shop in Broad Street (now a Wine Rack multiple).

Two social situations cannot readily be demonstrated in off-the-cuff talks: one was the prevalence of a male-orientated society; the other relates to the existence of a sharply defined class distinction, of which there were at least six cliques in our community – and woe betide you if you tried to climb from one into another!

In those far-away years when we had few cures and only about a dozen potent drugs, one's only justification for being a doctor was to take on one's own shoulders the burden of a patient's illness and the family's involvement and to be seen doing so.

E.C. Till, OBE

INTRODUCTION

Stamford: what a wonderful place in which to grow up and live! Thirty, forty, fifty and more years ago, the pace of life was slower than today but not a great deal has changed. It is true we have lost a station, but we have gained a north/south bypass. The swimming pool near the cattle market has gone and there is no longer a sheep market, but traffic is still a major problem despite the pedestrianization of the High Street. Change is inevitable but in Stamford it has not appeared too harsh. Perhaps this is because it is a conservation town and so has escaped many of the ravages of ugly urbanization.

This is a book of memories and recollections of life as it used to be. No longer is the town governed by the Blackstone Buzzer and I suspect fewer children learn to swim in the river at Gypsy Meadows or Cobbler's Hole these days. Dancing, either at local halls or at grand events, was once the main recreation in the town and there were regular visits to the cinema. Children were able to walk safely to school each day and set off on their bicycles with a picnic at weekends. Nobody locked the back door and groceries were delivered regularly with payment at the end of the week. What's more, shops had chairs to sit on while you waited to be served! Everyone I questioned spoke of hard work, long hours, trust and honesty – which does not mean that they were not up to mischief from time to time!

Most of the people whose memories are included in this book are retired and some are very elderly, yet their minds remain sharp and incisive. Remember that these are very personal recollections and some may differ considerably from others. Memory is fickle and has a nasty habit of being selective and changing with the years so if two people say things that are hugely different, then I am afraid it is up to you to choose whom you wish to believe!

The purpose of this book is, I believe, very important. Momentous and historic events happen during our lifetimes and they are duly recorded, but how people deal with these events and live through them is not. In recent years there has been a growing awareness of the importance of people's recollections of their childhood, working life, leisure time and entertainment, and how they coped during the First or Second World Wars. The pace of life has increased enormously in the past seventy or eighty years. Some of the people I met learnt to write in a sand tray or on a slate and now they see their grandchildren tapping away at computers. What a difference!

Recording past events from a personal point of view, as oral history, is now an accepted practice and regarded as an important addition to local and national archives. There are many local libraries and museums throughout the country which hold taped reminiscences of local people – indeed, our own museum has a collection – and a national body, the Oral History Society, was formed to promote and advise on this work.

Most people love talking about the past and once you start many memories come flooding back. I believe everyone I interviewed welcomed the opportunity to tell me about all the intricacies of life in Stamford during the early part of this century. It was a privilege to listen – even though, at times, there were some things I thought wiser not to include in the book! By listening to such memories of the past one has a better understanding of the present.

I have spoken to people at random and I think I am right in saying I knew only one contributor well and just a few by acquaintance, until I began this book. One person introduced me to the next and then someone else heard of what I was doing and contacted me. It has been very rewarding to find so many people who were willing to spend time with me. The bonus for me is that I have made many new friends!

Most people who have contributed to this book were born and have lived in Stamford all their lives although a few came to the town as youngsters. All have strong connections through family. However, I know there are gaps, which is inevitable in a book constructed in this way, and for that I apologize. People can only remember what they have experienced or learnt about from family and friends.

I hope this book will be useful to local historians and those researching their family histories as well as shedding further light on the social history of the town. There are some fine books written about the town as well as books of personal memories. I hope that this compilation of recollections will be a useful addition.

ACKNOWLEDGMENTS

My thanks go to all the people who have given their time to share their memories with me and who have lent me such evocative photographs to include in this book. For most of the thirteen photographs of the town lent by Stamford Museum, it has been impossible to trace the original ownership so we apologize if we have inadvertently infringed anyone's copyright. Staff at the Museum in Broad Street will be happy to discuss this and also to receive further donations of old photographs.

I am especially grateful to Dr Till for reading the manuscript and writing the Foreword, to Norman Haxell, who introduced me to many people and has been so enthusiastic about this book and to Richard Peoples for technical support.

Judith Spelman
Stamford
July 1999

CHAPTER 1

Early Memories

The Marquess of Exeter, then Mayor of Stamford, reading the Proclamation of the accession of King George V to the throne from the Town Hall Steps in 1910. Also shown are Charles Atter, Town Clerk, and mace-bearers Mr Lightfoot and Sergeant Carter. Mr Lightfoot, known as Matty, was 'the official wielder of the birch for recalcitrant boys'!

Women's Work

I was born at 38 Drift Gardens and lived there until I went into the Air Force to do my National Service. There were four of us, three sisters and myself. Life was not so easy in those days. I remember when my mother used a big square washing machine with a mangle on the back. There were no fridges but we had a meat safe in the pantry off the kitchen. We had quite a big garden so a lot of the vegetables came from the garden. When the council opened new allotments in Priory Road we had one of those.

Mick Warby

A Round Thing on Legs

My mother had a washing machine. It was a round thing on legs with a lever on the top and you had to move it up and down. My brother and I had to do that. It had paddles inside it. There was a hose that came from the tap and that filled it.

Eunice Sorfleet

Pulling Sheets

My mother had a copper in the back scullery and she used to boil the washing in that. We had a long garden to hang it out. Everything was washed by hand in those days and everything was thick and took a lot of drying. We used to fold and pull sheets to get them straight. My mother ironed with an old flat iron she had to put on the gas to heat.

Alice Burton

Travelling Home

My mother's parents lived in a cottage in Duncombe's Yard off Water Street. My first memories are getting on the Underground train in south-east London and travelling to King's Cross, getting on a steam train at King's Cross and getting off at Essendine and getting on to the train for Stamford. The station in Water Street was the Great Northern which was a branch line to Essendine.

Ernest Warner

Bowman's

I was born in St Mary's Street where there is still a stationer's shop. My father had a workshop in Wharf Road where he ran a painter and decorator's business. It was both house painting and a great deal of church decorating. Immediately after the First World War there was a great demand for war memorials. Bowman's built them and the Hares did the gold leaf and decorating. My grandfather was Edward Bowman who started his business in Bentley Street in 1886. My uncle moved the firm to its present site in Cherryholt Road in 1906. When I was a child we used to go to the workshops to play. They kept a great deal of wood, especially oak which had to be seasoned, and it was a fine place to play. There was always a lovely smell of wood.

Margaret Hare

Dig for Victory!

I lived in Doughty Street at the end of the 1920s and in those days it had eighteen houses which were only on one side. Then there was a gap, a piece of waste ground, then a hedge – a big, high hedge, another piece of waste ground and then two houses at the top end. Where the bungalow is now in Doughty Street there was a five-bar gate which went across the road. There was one path which went along in front of the houses while on the other side was rough ground. When we were youngsters we used to play on that.

In 1917, the war agricultural committee came and said they were

Frank Hare ran his decorating business from 39 St Mary's Street. He worked closely with Bowman's the builders.

E.S. Bowman on his motorcycle outside the Bowman works in Cherryholt Road.

11

going to plough that piece up and they told us they were putting it into sections. Each house was to have a section and we were to 'Dig for Victory'. They put a fence along the front.

Dick Grimwood

The Drift

Where the college is now there were allotments. As a boy I used to go to the top of Melbourne Road where there was a five-bar gate. I went through the gate and through the allotments and came to the Drift. There was Emlyn's Street at the top and Doughty Street and nothing in between. I think they started to build those houses on the Drift Road in about 1937.

Ernest Warner

Gypsy Meadows

We used to go down to the meadows behind Blackstone's on a summer afternoon. We used to paddle and I learnt to swim down there. We called that part Gypsy Meadows. At that time it was a much cleaner river and it was a really peaceful outing.

Mick Warby

Beautiful and Clean

We used to go swimming down in Gypsy Meadows. It was beautiful and clean there. Everybody went down there and if you weren't there by half

past one, you wouldn't get a place by the bank.

Freda Clark

Swinging over the River

Mum used to pull the reeds up and lash them together and they worked better than water wings. Some of the boys used to have a rope so that they could swing across the river. There used to be gangs of Teddy Boys and gangs of us girls but we all behaved ourselves!

Pamela Clark

She Managed

My mother was a war widow pensioner. She had £2 15s 5d per week and sometimes I wondered how she managed. We had quite a large garden and an unemployed uncle used to look after it. In the 1920s life was quiet. My father had left a good supply of books and I was quite a reader, or else I played with local children. We played cricket in the street and rounders. We'd go for walks and swam in the Uffington meadows and Gypsy Meadows behind Blackstones. Children were packed off there in the school holidays.

Ernest Warner

Living in Queen Street

My father, Fred Harris, was self-employed. He went and collected

The wedding of Fred Harris and Dora Hinson conducted by the Revd Wright at Barn Hill Methodist church in 1913. William Hinson, the builder, is second from the right.

eggs from the farmers in the villages around Stamford every Monday, Tuesday and Wednesday. On Thursdays he would go to Nottingham and sell them to the grocers' shops. I think he had a day off on Fridays because on Saturday mornings he would go to the villages and take one or two of us children with him. No more than two, though!

There were eight of us in our family – and only one boy. I was the fourth girl. They were hoping I'd be a boy and I was called Freda although my father always called me Fred. When my brother was born, he was named Fred William but was always called Bill.

We lived at 40 Queen Street and my father owned some land opposite so he had four houses built, numbers 15, 16, 17 and 18. We moved to number 18 which had a bit more land.

Freda Morse

The Rag Shop

The boys used to collect rags to take to the rag shop for money to spend at the fair. The people at the rag shop were called Lee and at one time it was where the public toilets are in Star Lane. Then it moved to the side of Marshall's Bakery in the High Street, where the Citizen's Advice Bureau is now. You'd probably get 3d for a bag of rags.

Freda Clark

13

Pennies in the Meter

Mr Croft used to come around at night to light the lamps in Doughty Street. He had a long pole and used to pull part of the lamp down to light it. I presume he came round and put them out but I never saw him. We lived on the old side of Doughty Street.
The houses were only built on one side and opposite were allotments and fields. The fields were all around, right up to Fane School. You could see the water tower up there if you looked out of the bedroom window.

We had gas lighting inside the house and we had to put pennies in the meter. I remember mum had a little jug and she put pennies in there. The lamps had funny mantles which had to be cleaned.

Alice Burton

Water Cart

When I was a boy all the goods that were sold were brought into the town by horses and carts. Consequently, there was a certain amount of excrement on the streets. So there was a man with a cart, which had a large container on it with two lids, one either side, and he used to walk round the streets and shovel up the excrement and take it away. Once a week a water cart came along and the streets were washed and cleaned by men with stiff brushes.

Richard (Dick) Grimwood

Room at the Inn

I was born in The Golden Fleece in Sheepmarket. My mother and father were Margaret and Henry Clarke. They went in first in 1900 and left in 1930. It is very different now from what it used to be. There was a big bar and a tap room. You went through the tap room to our living room which we called 'the little room' because it was so small. Upstairs there was a great big bedroom and three smaller bedrooms but there was no bathroom. We had a big tin bath we brought in at night and put by the fire. The WC was in the yard.

Because it was an inn, you were forced to take anyone who had nowhere to sleep for the night. The police used to bring people, often pedlars and hawkers. The big bedroom was shut off from the rest of the house and you got to it from the outside.

We used to play hopscotch, rounders and skipping outside. I remember the sheep being outside. They used to go up the road nearly as far as St Peter's Hill.

Margaret (Maggie) Graham

Two Types

My uncle used to tell me that there were two types of boys in the town – 'the muck boots' and the 'clean boots'!

Frank Riley

Young Organist

When we came to Stamford in 1925 we should have gone to St Mary's

The interior of St George's church in 1902.

church but we were in St George's parish and it was the habit then to go to your own parish church. That is where I first learnt to play the organ, when I was about fourteen. When I was learning I had to pay a small choirboy to pump the organ. By the end of the war most organs had been fitted with electric pumps.

Ernest Warner

Food for Thought

We used to eat a lot of liver when I was young but we were never allowed to have seconds!

Eunice Sorfleet

Butchering

As a child I used to visit the butcher's shop which was about four doors down from our house. Len Mould was the butcher and the slaughterhouse was behind the shop. He used to buy his sheep and bullocks down at the cattle market, drive them back to Scotgate and kill them behind the shop. As a small boy I was allowed to go in and watch.

Harold Harvey

Playing Together

All the children in our street played out, winter or summer. We were very free – no fear of abduction or being molested. Doors to our houses were never locked and neighbours helped each other out. Everybody seemed to be as well off as the next person. I remember being given second-hand clothes from the girl across the road. I was glad – they were quite fashionable!

Pamela Clark

Cigarette Cards

I was born in Princes Road and we moved to Easton for a couple of years and then down to Priory Road. After that, Mum and Dad had a house built in Empingham Road. There was nothing there but two bungalows and a laundry. We used to climb trees on Roman Bank. On one side there were allotments and on the other side there were fields.

We used to collect cigarette cards which had pictures of sports personalities and army people. There were albums to stick them in. We used to ride our bikes around the countryside because it was very safe then. When we were at school we used to go to the swimming baths but after school we used to go down to the river.

Jimmy Jackson

Floods

We used to get a lot of floods and the water came up Castle Dyke. At the bottom was a dairy – Booth's dairy. When Mrs Booth got elderly, her daughter and her husband took it over and they were Musgroves. On the opposite side was part of the old castle but they've built houses there now. We left The Golden Fleece when I was eleven years old and went to live at 31 Recreation Ground Road. When I was seventeen we moved to 18 St George's Street, next to where The White Hart used to be.

Maggie Graham

Keeping Pigs

Our orchard was extended to the top of Rock Road and at the top my father erected a pig sty. It was very useful because the leftover food from the bakery went to feed the pigs. At Christmas we killed one of our own pigs and my memory is of the butcher coming round to our garden, stringing up the pig and killing it.

Harold Harvey

Out and About

We used to cycle a lot and there was no problem because there weren't that many cars.

Doris Borowik

Away Days

When we were children we went picnicking at the Barnack Hills and Holes and to Fineshade. We would take pork pies with us. We would go to

Hunstanton or Skegness which were about sixty miles away and could be done quite comfortably in a day. We would walk along the beach and swim if we could. When we got to King's Lynn we were usually able to calculate whether the tide would be in or out. When it got dark we had to light the lamps on the car.

Margaret Hare

Changing the Rules

As a boy I remember playing shove ha'penny and bagatelle quite a bit! We used to have sessions of Monopoly in the school holidays that lasted for days. That was probably because we used to allow borrowing which isn't in the rules.

Michael Tebbutt

Jam Sandwiches

I liked to eat jam sandwiches which I was allowed to take over to a relative's who had a son who was two and a half years younger than me. He and I had a tent in the garden and we used to eat them in there. I had a school friend and she sometimes joined us. We played all sorts of games and climbed trees and had great fun.

Margaret Hare

Bar of Chocolate

We weren't allowed to knit on a Sunday or go biking. Probably we were given a bar of chocolate to eat. We had big dolls we used to play with and we did embroidery too.

Mary Munton

CHAPTER 2
Schooldays

The Fane School. Kathleen Musson, now Walker, is on the right in the back row.

The Old Coke Stove

I went to St George's School down Wharf Road where Jessop's is. The yard where they put the cars was the playground. There were a lot of us in the class – over forty – and we used to share books between three of us. In the corner of the classroom there was an old coke stove. If you sat near it you were warm but it was cold if you were across the room. Mum wrote one day asking if I could sit near it because I had a cold. The teachers were very interested in us and I don't think there was one person who left there who couldn't read and write.

Pamela Clark

Looking at Sweets

When we moved to Stamford I was sent to the Bluecoat School which was in All Saints Street. We had a council house in Melbourne Road and to me it was beautiful because south Bermondsey was a very drab area. In Melbourne Road we had the school field at the back and what struck me most were all the places you could go. There were meadows all over Stamford! I use to walk to school four times a day and I used to stop and look in Harvey's shop window at the sweets.

Ernest Warner

'It didn't pay'

I first went to Brazenose School in St Paul's Street which was an easy walk from Maiden Lane where we lived. Mrs Granger was one of the teachers and there was Miss Kelford whose father was a shoemaker, Miss Langley and Miss Smith. Miss Evelyn Thomas was the headmistress. It closed about 1928. I remember my father saying it didn't pay. Then I went to St George's and after that you either went to the Bluecoat School or St Michael's.

Frank Riley

Sergeant Stiff giving road safety instructions to schoolgirls in St Peter's Street, 1945/46.

The Bluecoat School. Frank Riley is second from the right, back row.

A Circular Washbasin

I went to the Fane School first which is now Queen Eleanor. Miss Wright was my first teacher. The thing that amazed me was a great big circular washbasin with sprinklers all the way round. The school was a long line of single-storey classrooms and they followed round with a veranda so it went into an L-shape. This washbasin was in the washroom in the top corner. I seem to remember somebody taking a banana to school and it was the first one I had ever seen. It was about 1943. It dropped out of a boy's pocket and somebody stood on it.

Mick Warby

A Lifetime Interest

I was born in the house where I still live. I first went to the kindergarten at the High School and then I went to Stamford School. We were taught at the kindergarten by Miss Betty Batty who was very pleasant and introduced me to mythology which has been a lifetime interest. Two of the High School girls used to call for me and walk me to school – about a mile and a half. We all sat at small desks.

Stuart Rodgers

Air-Raid Practice

At the Fane School there was an air-raid shelter in the school grounds.

We had air-raid practice, when we had to line up and march down to the shelter.

Eunice Sorfleet

Cooking Yorkshire Puddings

St Augustine's School was in Broad Street. We had three teachers; the headmistress was Miss Poole and there was Miss McLauchlan, who got married and became Mrs Harvey, and Miss Walker was the infant teacher.

When I first started we wore skirts and dresses but after a few years we had to wear gymslips. We used to do mental arithmetic, sewing and reading. The first thing we did in the mornings was the catechism and religious instruction. We would go swimming and on a Friday afternoon we used to go to cookery lessons in the Technical School across the road. I can remember cooking Yorkshire puddings and we made bread and marmalade. While we were at cooking, the boys used to go to woodwork in a building at the back of the Technical School.

Over the top of the Technical School there used to be the nurse who came round the schools and when the school dentist came, he was in the same part. So was the optician.

My friend, Eva Hibbins, lived where Candlesticks in St Martins is now. There was a passage that used to go from there to Wothorpe Road but it was blocked up. I left school at fourteen and went to work at the fish shop in Cheyne Lane.

Maggie Graham

Nine Years

I went to St Augustine's Catholic school in Broad Street. I went there when I was five and finished there when I was fourteen. Canon West used to come into the school and we had to stand and say 'Good morning, Father West.' He used to wear black gaiters and a black hat and children would always get a halfpenny off him.

Doris Borowik

Writing Tools

We went in for handwriting competitions. They used to bring the inkwells round. The ink was made with powder and water and the inkwells were put in holes in the desk. The pens were wood and you had to fix the nib on the end.

Pamela Clark

Writing on Slates

We learnt to write on slates using a slate pencil. They were about A4 size with a wooden frame. The monitor would give them out. I don't remember how they cleaned them – probably spat on them!

Ellis Miles

Friends for Life

I went to St George's School which was on Wharf Road. Doris Beales (now Rowton) and I were there together and

Millicent Eayrs (seated, front row), headmistress of St George's School who retired in 1921, with Edith Wilcox (centre) and Lavinia Eayrs.

we've been friends since we were five years old. Mrs Shaw was the headmistress and there was Miss Bland and Miss Harper. We used to go to the Technical School for cookery lessons with Miss Harrison. There was one girl who couldn't break an egg and they used to hand it round the backs of the girls to me to break. We made fruit cakes and sponges.

Alice Burton

Dancing in St Mary's Street

I was never still when I was young. I was always doing something. I used to go to Mrs Staveley Parker's to do tap dancing. She and Dr Staveley Parker lived in St Mary's Street but we used to do our tap dancing at the Girl Guides' hut in Conduit Street. Sometimes two or three of us went to her house because she had a big mirror in one of the rooms and we could see ourselves dancing.

Doris Borowik

I started school at the Fane School which is now Queen Eleanor. My mother took me the first day to the infants' there. I don't think I liked or disliked it. I remember coming home one day during morning playtime thinking school was over, I was quickly despatched back again by my mother.

There was no uniform when we started but we were all neat and tidy. We wore a blouse, skirt and cardigan. We had white socks and lace up shoes or shoes with a button across. In winter we wore long socks up to our knees. Mother made us garters to keep them up.

We had a teacher called Miss Musson who I remember as a very kind lady. The whole class had a photograph taken with her and she was wearing a pink cardigan with many buttons down the front which fascinated me. Miss Bonello was the headmistress. She was very elegant and very well dressed and she had a nice speaking voice. There was no bullying in those days. At our school there were different sorts of desks and we sat in rows. Some were single desks and some were double, with lids that lifted up to put books inside.

Pamela Clarke

'Lukies'

I went to a marvellous little dame school in St Peter's Street which was kept by two old ladies – the Misses Luke. People used to call it 'Lukies'. It consisted of two rooms. A big room was for children up to about nine and the little room was for the younger ones. It was very 'ritualistic' and we played quoits every break time. At the end of every term every child had a prize with a Biblical card which had a decoration on and a text.

There was one awful term when one of the boys had been so naughty that they had to deprive him of his prize. He was allowed to have the card, though. Once when the big children were sitting round the huge table, he got under it. The older Miss Luke, who was very fierce, was trying to get him out with a stick, but he wouldn't come out.

I was learning Latin at seven and French irregular verbs. Every night we had to learn a verse of the Bible and repeat it first thing next morning. This was horrific because I hated learning by heart and I was very bad at it.

We learnt to write in lined copybooks. There was a sample line at the top and the writing was sloping. We wrote with pen and ink although we probably had pencils at first.

Sheila Miles

A Walk before School

When I was at Stamford High School there was a small number of boarders and they each had their own cubicle where they slept rather than being in a large dormitory. Every morning they had a walk before school began. When I left there were only about 200 girls there. My great friend at school was Joyce Warburton who lived in Adelaide Street. Her father was a stationmaster.

Margaret Hare

Three Schools

I went to St John's School and then to All Saints' in Austin Street and then I went to the Fane School. I was one of the first to go there. There used to be a school in Empingham Road. We were never taught the things they learn today. We did mental arithmetic. We sat at double desks but in St John's we sat on chairs. I used to love doing cookery.

Kath Walker

Warm Milk

I went to St George's Junior School after leaving the Fane Infants'. This time we had a uniform. It was a blue gymslip and a red tie. It was a very old building on Wharf Road and it was very cold. Our class teacher was Mrs Banning and she taught us English and country dancing which we performed at the school fête. Mrs Halford was my favourite teacher and she taught English.

We had milk to drink in the morning. It came in little bottles and we were given straws. Sometimes it was put close to the radiators and it was lukewarm. We all walked to school and if it was raining we still had to sit in our wet clothes all day. When I started at St George's School we were encouraged to save regularly. I would take sixpence every Monday to put in the school bank. It soon added up. If we went on a school trip we would pay weekly. Once we went to London Zoo. It was going to cost 19s 11d so we took a shilling a week for twenty weeks.

I remember one girl, Betty Haddon, fell over and cut her hand badly so we all had

Stamford School rugby team, 1948/49. From left to right, back row: E. Smith, I.C. Rock, J.D. Clark, M.H. Woods, J.H. Savage, J.G. Harrison, R.E. Corby, A. Jessop. Middle row: W.R. Burchnall, K. Buckley, R.E. Pearce (captain), Mr H.E. Packer, N. Miller, D.H. Murphy. Sitting in front: M.J.K. Smith, N.C. (Colin) Dexter, D.L. Gilbert. M.J.K. Smith was later to be captain of the England cricket team and also played rugby for the national side.

Stamford School choir outside the Town Hall after the first broadcast from Stamford which took place at The George Hotel on 27 April 1935. Mrs Tinkler, the teacher who first taught Malcolm Sargent to play the piano, is in the centre of the third row from the top.

to wait in a huddle while they rushed her off to hospital and she came back with three stitches. I can't remember which bus service was used to take us to London. It could have been the Cream Bus Service which was run by Mr W.H. Patch and operated in the town. It had slatted wooden seats and it wasn't very comfortable.

My father, Eric Clark, went to St George's when he was young.

Pamela Clark

Learning to Swim

I learnt to swim when I was at school. We used to go to the swimming baths and they used to put you on a rope and they used to pull you along. During the holidays I taught myself because we spent a lot of time there. We used to go swimming down to the meadows. It was beautiful down there and we all used to meet and picnic. And then the little boy was drowned and mother didn't want us to go. We would walk up as far as Easton one week and then to Tinwell the next week.

Doris Borowik

Whetting the Appetite

We used to go to the swimming pool and Mr Pashler taught us to swim. He used to put a halter round our tummies and take us up and down. Then one day you realized he hadn't got the rope and you were swimming. I used to go with the school. I wanted to go every day which would have cost half a crown so my mother bought me a season ticket. We used to walk back from the pool and we were that hungry! I can smell the baking from Neve and Parsley's now!

Alice Burton

Champion

I was champion swimmer at Stamford School and I used to swim for the county and when I was in the R.A.F. I used to swim with Stamford Swimming Club before the baths were built and they used to race in the Meadows. They erected platforms so that they could swim there for competitions, going up towards the iron footbridge before you get to the A1. The swimming pool we had at last was built where the cattle market car park now is.

Pamela Clark in her uniform at St George's School.

The headmistress of Stamford High School, Miss Nichol (seated), with, from left to right, Miss Best, Miss McIntosh and Miss Eldridge.

We tried our hardest to persuade the council to have it covered but they would not do it. When they did decide to cover it in they ordered a cover, which cost enough, and when it came it was the wrong size!

Grahamme Sorfleet

Scholarship

The first school I went to was St John's Infants' School which was at the bottom of West Street. It was run by a Miss Dale. Barbara and Moira Patch were twins in my form. Then I went to The Bluecoat School where the headmaster was J.C.H. 'Johnny' Taylor who lived in Queen Street. When I was eleven I won a scholarship to the grammar school when I met the Reverend J.D. Day who was headmaster of the school and lasted a long time. 'Savage Parsons March Black Tye

Miles Long' was a sentence we made of boys' names in my form.

Ellis Miles

Handy with the Cane

I went to St John's Primary School, the Blue Coat School and then St Michael's School and one of my teachers was Mr Ward. I remember him because he used to have a red face and we called him Oxo! And there was Mr Sylvester. The headmaster at St Michael's was named Mr Niblet. He did not like me and I certainly did not like him! He was very handy with the cane. The curriculum included carpentry which took place at the back of the Technical School in Broad Street, and gardening. The school gardens were substantial and were at the rear of St Michael's. We each used to have a garden plot and grew vegetables.

Terence Asker

Left Handed

When I was at St Michael's School the headmaster told my teacher to send me to him every morning at nine o'clock. I used to go and he'd tell me to put my left hand out and he'd give me one stroke across the palm of my hand with the cane. That was to stop me writing with my left hand. When I first went to the school I was writing left handed and he said it was a rule of his school that everyone wrote with the right hand. That was Mr Markwick who used to live opposite the Grammar School at number 32 St Paul's Street. But he was a good man. Later on as I went from class to class I finished up with eight to ten others in his private room at the back of his office. He gave us lectures and talks about all sorts of things.

Dick Grimwood

Boys and Trunks

The Eastern Railway used to go to Essendine. It was a bit of a push and pull job with two carriages. At the beginning and end of every term the entire train was packed solidly with boys and trunks. Fewer people brought children to school by car.

Michael Tebbutt

Grahamme Sorfleet dives into the old swimming pool near the cattle market.

Those Were the Days

I never locked my back door. Nobody did. I would go to town and leave it unlocked in case the children came back from school before I did.

Freda Clark

Showing Promise

The first thing I ever did on the stage was in 1938 when I was Britannia at St Martin's School when they did a pageant. St Martin's School was the corner building on the turning into Wothorpe Road. I was at the Bluecoat School, which in those days was where the Masonic Centre now is in St Peter's Street, and because they were short of pupils at St Martin's, they divided the town so that the children on that side went to the school. That was in the 1930s.

Grahamme Sorfleet

Combining the Schools

I taught at St Gilbert's School when it was by the traffic lights in Scotgate. It's now All Saints and St John's community centre. That was the infant department and the junior department was in Austin Street. In the early 1970s, a combined school was built in Foundry Road. We used to use the Ladybird Series of books for reading.

Helen Grace

Sliding down the Drift

The Drift, when I was a boy, was a cart track. There were gutters, about nine inches deep, and in the winter time they were full of ice. Going to school, you could slide from Doughty Street right to where the college gate is now at the foot of the hill. I used to go up the Drift when I went to St Michael's School.

Dick Grimwood

Keep Off the Grass

I went back to the Fane School as a secondary student. There was a uniform of navy skirt, white blouse and a red tie. Miss Yates was the headmistress. She was a very tough lady who I was terrified of! Mr Hunt was the school caretaker and he wasn't a man to be trifled with. The school had a large area of grass which he looked after with loving care and woe betide anybody who walked on it. I still remember him shouting at me many times to get off the grass!

Miss Cropley was one of my favourite teachers and she took us for history and always made the lessons interesting. Our sights were always set on academic subjects. Miss Yates thought athletics a waste of time so we had one pair of spiked running shoes which were worn by whoever made the grade to represent the school. Most of us stayed on at school to do typing or shorthand. Blackstones took most of the girls for clerical work and the boys became apprentices.

Pamela Clark

Mr Ellis and his woodwork class from St Michael's School, 1913/15.

Colourful

I remember sewing a lime green nightdress which was almost square. It was a lovely lime green but had no shape to it. It was all hand sewn because we never had machines. We had to sew double seams which took a long time. They were called run and fell seams. I also remember making a violet-mauve apron!

Mary Munton

Blue Overalls

When I first went to school I was four and a half. We wore little blue overalls with red embroidery at the edges. We sat around in little groups on stools at the end of the day and were told stories. Sometimes we would fetch a tray and be given wet clay to play with. Our exercise books were in squares and we were allowed to crayon in the squares and make different patterns. On very fine days in the summer we sometimes went for a walk and we picked wild flowers from the hedges.

Margaret Hare

Prayers Every Day

I went to Brazenose School before the Grammar School took it. Miss Harper was my teacher and I was about six when I went there. We were living in Melbourne Road so it wasn't far to go. There was a lassie who lived at number 15 and she used to take me. My mother wouldn't let me go to school until I was six and they didn't know about me until she wanted me vaccinated and then they found out about me! Then I went on to the High School when Miss Nichol was the head. We always started the day with prayers.

Mary Munton

Centenary celebrations at Stamford High School, May 1977. The headmistress at the time was Miss Margaret Medcalf.

CHAPTER 3
Working Life

Harry Warby, who worked at Edmondson's
Electrical Company for over forty years.

Bert Sorfleet after the Second World War, when he worked for Clark and Belton in St Paul's Street.

Taking out the Gas Lamps

My father used to work at the electricity board when they had generators at Wharf Road. I think they were known as Edmondson's Electrical Company. He worked there for probably forty-four years and he saw things change. He went on with Mid Lincs Electricity Board and East Midlands Electricity Board when they took over the old sheds where the generators and great big diesel were kept. When the grid came in they closed all the generators down. My dad was working for the electricity board when I left school so he saw the manager and I got a job there to do an apprenticeship. I earned 9d an hour. At that time we were often taking gas lights out and putting electric lights in. Since then I have rewired some of those houses. They used to do a system

John Thomas Warby worked for Gooch, the veterinary surgeon, in the early 1900s.

Esther or Effie Warby was a district nurse in Stamford for many years. This picture was taken in December 1940.

called capping and casing. It was a wooden channel which was screwed on the wall and the wires would fit in the slots and go to porcelain ceiling roses and brass lamp holders. We were taking that sort of thing out and using rubber sheathed cables then.

Mick Warby

The Buzzers

Blackstone's and Miles's buzzers used to go off to let people know it was time for work. Blackstones would go at twenty past seven and half past, then again at mid-day and ten to one and one o'clock. There was always a ten minute warning. I won't swear to it but I think Miles's buzzer went at twelve-thirty. I can see George Miles now, standing in his warehouse coat at the office door.

Frank Riley

Nobody Took Any Notice!

I remember the morning when they pedestrianized the High Street. Cars were rushing into the street. There used to be a barrier near Wilkos but nobody took any notice!

Frank Riley

Winding the Clocks

We used to wind all the clocks at Burghley House. I don't know how many there were but it used to take a morning. I remember my father used to say he was always a bit worried when he was winding the turret clock in case the click-spring broke and then the click would give way and the whole thing would fly back. He was always glad when that was over. He used to go on a Tuesday morning and he did this for eighteen years. If Tuesday happened to be Christmas Day he still went; if it was thick snow, he still went. He never missed. He also went twice a year to put the clocks forward for British Summer Time and then back again in the autumn.

When I came back from the war, he was taken ill with Bell's Palsy and was told to go home and rest for six months. I had to run the shop and on Tuesday morning I thought to myself, am I to close the shop and go and wind Burghley clocks or not? I decided I had better find out what we were charging. I looked it up and found we were charging 2s 3d a week! I thought it was not worth it because I could not afford to close the shop for that amount – which incidentally, included the two free visits to put the clocks forwards or backwards. Mind you, my father had carte blanche to keep the clocks going so if one needed overhauling, he'd bring it home with him – usually on the back of his bicycle.

Stuart Rodgers

A Bypass in 1939

There was a bypass proposed for Stamford in 1939. It was not so much a bypass as a relief road and it was going to come down Wothorpe Road, across the meadows, up through the Millstone yard and somehow into Scotgate. The clerk of the works was ready to start and he'd set his office up here in Stamford but the war came and the plans were abandoned. They had built a 'hump' on the meadows which was here for years before they levelled it off.

Frank Riley

Chicken Coops

Frank Storey ran some of the buses. They ended up as chicken coops.

Mark Hooson

Errand Boy

I worked as an errand boy at the Star Tea Store which was on the corner of Silver Lane and the High Street. When I finished school about four I went there and worked until about six. On Saturdays I was there all day. I had a trolley which had two wheels which I pushed.

Dick Grimwood

Odds and Evens

Parking in the High Street. It was done on dates. On even dates you parked on one side of the road and on

Charles Rodgers, who in 1929 opened his business as a watchmaker and jeweller in Red Lion Square, next to the Midland Bank, now HSBC.

odd dates you parked on the other. In the Sixties they put the 'sausage' into Red Lion Square. By that I mean the curved pavement which divides off the parking area. The square used to be completely open space with a huge, elegant, three-pronged gas lamp in the middle.

Mark Hooson

Testing Tubes

When I left school I worked as a waitress at Neve and Parsley's in Red Lion Square. I wasn't there very long because of the war and I had to go and work in Cascelloid's which was opposite to Somerfield's. Mr Higgins and Mr Richardson used to work there. I used to test the tubes they made but it was all very secret. Mrs Town and Betty Baker worked there. They moved the factory to where Somerfield's is. I left when my first child was born.

Kath Walker

Thirty-eight Years an Organist

My mother came from Belmesthorpe and after my father died we came to live in Stamford in 1925. Apart from my war service and one term teaching in Oxford, I spent the rest of the time teaching at Deacon's School in Peterborough. My first organ job was at St Michael's church. I was asked by Canon Day to play the organ at St Martin's church. I went in 1952 and I retired in 1990. I was an organist at St Martin's for thirty-eight years.

Ernest Warner

Plum Pud

My mother, whose maiden name was Rippin, was born at Stoke Doyle. She cooked by a three-burner Valor Perfection oil stove. She was a very good cook and my favourite was plum pudding. She used to be a cook at Rock Lodge in Empingham Road which belonged to Mr Halliday the builder. That's where my father met her.

Frank Riley

Train Travelling

I used to travel by train to Peterborough. The first train was 7.30 in the morning from Water Street. We changed at Essendine and were into Peterborough at five minutes past eight. There was no train from the Midland station that early. I had a season ticket for each term which cost me £7 10s and you could use it on either route. I used to go from Water Street and come back on the Midland route that went on to Leicester. They closed the Water Street station, or Stamford East station to give it its proper name, in 1959. Colloquially, the two stations were known as the Northern and the Midland. In 1910 there were fifteen steam trains a day from Stamford to Essendine and fifteen back.

There used to be a through carriage

Sidney Allen outside the George Tap in 1912 with one of Stamford's first horse buses. They were kept in the stables at the George Hotel and used for taking people and goods to and from the old Great Northern station. It cost sixpence to the centre of town. Mr Allen drove the parcel bus and worked from seven in the morning until nine at night. The photograph shows the landlord of the George Tap, Fred Clarke, on the right.

from King's Cross to Water Street every day. It left King's Cross at 5 o'clock, stopped at Hitchin where the first part went on to Cambridge and the second part carried on up the main line calling at Huntingdon and Peterborough and Essendine. At Essendine, the local engine was attached to the carriage and brought it on to Stamford. In the late 1930s there was one very good train scheduled at 8.37 in the morning and arrived at 10.28 at King's Cross. That was very good for those days.

Ernest Warner

Delivery Boy

When I was about thirteen I was a grocery boy. I worked at the Co-op. I started in Doughty Street. The job was promised to me before I was thirteen. I was thirteen on the Friday and I started on the Monday. I was there for two weeks and the boy at the High Street branch went on holiday so they sent me there. When this lad came back, the manager was in a quandary what to do but they gave me the job. It was nearer for me to go from St Michael's School which was at the bottom of 'Rec' Road.

I spent half my time in the warehouse and the rest delivering groceries. We used to put the sugar into bags. There would be a line of us; I'd be filling, someone else would be weighing, and the next person would be closing the bag. They used to do the same thing with soap. Currants, sultanas and raisins used to come in wooden boxes to be weighed out. I used to go straight there and work till six. I took the orders out to customers that were too late to go on the van.

In the shop there was a lady in a small office who took all the money. The sales assistant would put the money into a little wooden cup and screw it to a holder on a wire up high, pull a handle and it would shoot across the shop to this office. The cashier would unclip it, count it, and send any change back.

Mick Warby

Miles and Blackstones

My husband, Stanley Graham was a local man and he was in the Merchant Navy on HMS *Grenville*. When he first started work he went to Miles' wood yard which was near the main railway station. They've built houses there now. When he was twenty and we got engaged he thought he'd better go where the wages were a bit better so he went to Blackstones where he worked until he went into the forces. When he came out of the Navy he went back to working at Blackstones.

Maggie Graham

Congestion in the High Street before pedestrianization. (copyright: *Stamford Mercury*)

Red Lion Square with its central lamp standard, c. 1922.

Timber

At Miles's all the timber was on the left-hand side with the saw benches. The stables were that side too. They used to go out into the country to fetch the timber and it went in at one end onto the saw benches. Behind them was Godfrey's the timber merchants and they made sheds.

Dick Grimwood

Busy with Traffic

I clearly remember the days when the A1 ran straight through the town, right through St Mary's Street, over the town bridge and past The George and away out again. I worked for the electricity company and we had offices in Barn Hill and a showroom on St Mary's Street. There was just traffic, traffic, traffic along St Mary's Street in

those days. Buses would come straight through the High Street down to Red Lion Square and turned right or left. When the High Street paving was laid – that was done with Stamford bricks, of course – I am almost certain that this was the first town in the country to have its main street pedestrianized.

The High Street was so busy with traffic. We used to have a cricket team and when we went off to play other teams we used to play cards in the bus to pass the time. I remember coming in from Market Deeping, along St Paul's Street and then crawl through the High Street. We forgot the cards once and when the bus on which we were sat was stopped along the High Street, Ron Lewis jumped off, went into the stationers and bought a pack of cards. And still the bus hadn't moved when he got back! The traffic used to get snarled up in Red Lion Square – it would back up all the way round St Mary's Street to Red Lion Square. I lived a mile and a

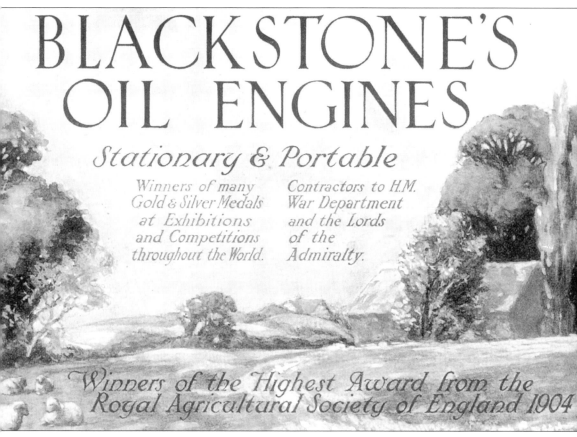

Blackstone's advertisement.

half out of town but I used to walk to work every day.

Sid Hall

The Gas Lamp

Red Lion Square always used to be full of cars or carts and in the middle was a great gas lamp.

Ellis Miles

The Laundry

I worked at the Stamford Steam Laundry for twenty-four years. That was up the Empingham Road on the left-hand side. There are houses built on the site now. The laundry arrived in bags and hampers. We did laundry for the Peterborough hospitals and for Brudenells of Deene. At one time the laundry belonged to people in Stamford but they sold it to Belgraves of Leicester and they were who I worked for.

There were different jobs for everyone. There was a big roller to do the sheets and tablecloths all went through. The laundry was brought in and put in separate piles. One girl had a machine and stamped an

BLACKSTONE'S SWATH TURNERS

Haymakers, Horse Rakes.

Blackstone's Patent Swath Turners won the 1st Prize of £15 and Silver Medal, also the Second Prize of £10 and Bronze Medal.

Blackstone's Patent Side Delivery Rake Won the First Prize of £15 and Silver Medal,

at the Royal Agricultural Society of England's Competitive Field Trials at Lincoln 1907.

identifying number on it so it wouldn't get mixed up. I was in the sorting room and I was supervisor. There were four girls in a row and as they did each person's laundry they used to put it on the conveyor belt and I used to sort it and put it in different barrow for the wash-house. There were sheets in one, tablecloths in another, towels in another and so on. Then the lad from the wash house would come and wheel the barrow out when they were full. There were about four van men who went around and collected the laundry.

We always had to go through the pockets before things were washed and we used to find watches and rings and money – which was always sent back to the owner. When the laundry was closed I went to work for BT in Foundry Road and I've worked for Asker's for eight years.

Kath Walker

Blue and Red

My great-grandfather began the Blackstone works. When they first started they made mostly farm machinery which was always painted blue and red. They had a showroom in Broad Street on the corner, which then was bought by the Central Cinema.

Doreen Blackstone

Huge Diesels

Blackstone's made huge diesel engines. You had to stand on a platform to read the exhaust temperature. I worked with Dickie Witt who was the engineer.

Jimmy Jackson

Cars

Father used to pick me from school on his way from work. I can remember the front of the works on Ryhall Road. There was a large window and a big shiny engine behind it. We used to have a great big green Rover which was open topped. It never would start so we would push it out of the garage and down the hill to get it going. At the works they had an Armstrong Siddeley which was a square sort of car. We used to go to Brampton Races in that because you could sit on the top and see more.

Doreen Blackstone

First Car

The first car I bought was a Ford Consul. I paid £716 14s 11d. The problem was getting a car because there were usually long waiting lists. I went to a dealer called Motors and Tractors who had an office in St John's Street. The salesman at the time was Ernest Betts. I asked how long was the waiting list and he said I could have the next car that came in. A few weeks went by and there was no sign of a car so I went to see him and was told none had come in. This went on and on until one day a man I knew came to see me and said he had just come past Motors and Tractors' depot near the railway station and they had just had thirty-four Consuls delivered. I went straight down on my bicycle and asked which one was mine! We're very sorry, they said, but these are all going to sub-agents. Then a week or so later I was talking in the shop to a traveller and he said I should go up to London. Apparently the show rooms were full. So I rang Motors and Tractors up and said if there was not a car in my garage that night I would cancel my order! It arrived!

The first day I sat in it I pulled a knob and it came off. We managed to get it going and I went to see a friend across the valley and on the way back the air filter fell across the sparking plugs and shorted them out. I rolled to a stop and had to get a garage to sort it out. And so it went on.

One day I was coming home from work and in the garage down the street was the most gorgeous thing I had ever seen: an MG Magnet saloon. I had it for thirteen years. It was British racing green and unusually, it was fitted with everything. My best friend had a Sunbeam Rapier which was a very pretty car in black and yellow. It had the very latest attachments, including overdrive.

Stuart Rodgers

The Finishing School

When I left school I went to be an apprentice draftsman at Blackstone's. This meant that I spent a year going through the Works. We started every day with the buzzer and if you were five minutes late you lost that morning. The gates were locked. Blackstone's was the main employer in the town in those days. I was fifteen when I went to work there. I had a longer apprenticeship than most because I was sent up to the Shetland Islands during the war. I was there for six months and it was part of my practical experience. I had to help put in power houses at RAF stations.

In those days you weren't a draftsman until you were twenty five – and you kept your nose clean. My mother always called Blackstone's 'The Finishing School'. They were hard taskmasters but very fair. When I worked for Blackstone's it was run by Major Pratt. The main offices then were at Dursley. We are talking about 1938 here.

I moved on to Martin's who made agricultural machinery and dairy boilers and equipment. It was a very small firm and I was the only draftsman so I did everything. In those days the directors were Trevor Jones and Howard Jones.

Jimmy Jackson

Moving at Night

Dowmac, the cement people, used to transport all the big girders for the bridges to go over the A1 down the High Street in the night. They were so long you couldn't transport them during the day.

Alice Burton

Working at Froment's

The war came along and you couldn't get things and sweets and chocolate were rationed so my parents sent me out to work. I went to Froment's in the High Street. It was where the electrical shop and Wand's is now. They sold everything – hats, coats, dresses, coconut matting, oil cloth, baize, pinafores, blankets, sheets, haberdashery. I used to be ever so proud of the haberdashery. We had all the coloured cottons imaginable and beautiful ribbons at the beginning of the war. As the war went on we didn't get many in. The tailors and the dressmakers used to come in and, oh dear, they would fiddle about for ages looking for exactly what they wanted. There were a lot of dressmakers and tailors here then.

When people bought coconut matting they used to want it binding. It really hurt our fingers. We used a hessian binding and we had to sew it on one side and turn it over the raw edge and sew it the other side. Then we rolled it up and tied it and put a label on it and I had to take it down to the bus. I had to go through the town carrying it. I used to feel so embarrassed!
I had to work so hard there but I only got 7s 6d a week. I had to wear black and I had black hair so I thought I looked terrible! There was only one other person working there and Mr and Mrs Froment. We had to work so hard. There was nobody to clean. I had to roll the carpets up and get them downstairs and out into the yard and then I'd get the yard brush and sweep them.

They had a boiler in the kitchen and in the winter I had to rake it out and try and start it. Once I'd got it going we'd have cocoa and then I'd go into Broad

Street, get my bike and go round to people's houses collecting 6d club money. That would take me until twelve o'clock. The next day I'd do another area. At the end of the year they used to come into the shop to spend however much they had collected on their cards and they would be given a discount. You could spend all the afternoon with a customer.

There was also an oil stove and I used to clean the wick, fill it up with paraffin and put it in the shop downstairs. Then about dinner time, I'd carry it, alight, up the stairs to where we sold the coats and dresses. I was about fifteen at the time and I didn't think anything of it! I used

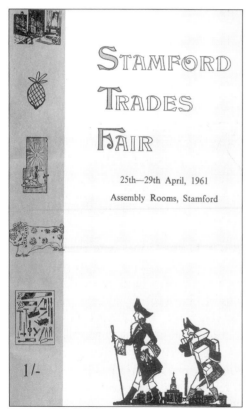

Stamford Trades Fair, organized by the Chamber of Trade, took place in the Assembly Rooms in 1961.

to go down into the cellar and chop some sticks.

Doris Borowik

Trade Fair

There was a custom to hold an annual trade fair in the Arts Centre prior to its modernization. All the prominent tradesmen in the town would rent a small stand. The whole of the ballroom would be occupied and there would be a spill-over into the Blue Room. I was asked to do the electrical work there for a few years.

Sid Hall

Only One Department

When I left Froment's – and I was there about three years – I went to the underwear department of Oates & Musson's. It was such a difference. There was me with only the underwear department to see to! I just dusted and then there was nothing else. I'd just sit down and wait for customers to come in. Oates & Musson's and Seccombe's in St Mary's Street were the shops. Seccombe's was where John Sinclair is now.

Doris Borowik

The Smell of Wood

It was an interesting area around the station before they started building all those houses. It smelled nice because of the wood being sawn in the wood yard. There were some big wooden structures which housed the saw and steam engine and there were lots of elm and oak logs stacked high. They never seemed to change. Beyond there was a tall warehouse of orange brick which was very little used. There was also a coal merchant. The station was always busy. You'd see crates of chickens or pigeons on the platforms. There was also a bookstall on the station.

Ellis Miles

Steaming On

You could get a train to Harwich from Stamford station.

Sheila Miles

Haulage Firm

The main part of Welland Mews when we first moved to Stamford was the east railway which ran parallel to the river for between $\frac{1}{2}$ and $\frac{3}{4}$ mile when it turned and went across the water and on to Essendine. It was still in use at the time. After this station was closed, the area was used for a long time by haulage contractors.

Sid Hall

Mushroom Growers

Cuttings used to make compost for mushroom growing in Water Street and distribute it all over the country

from here. Before that it used to be the site of Hunt's Brewery. There were cottages on the riverbank where the gardens are.

Sid Hall

A Complete House Furnisher

On 31 December 1962 I started work for Wilfred Bontoft at 30 High Street in Stamford. He described himself as 'a complete house furnisher'. He had come to the town from Yorkshire and worked at Oates & Musson's. I started on six months' trial with him.

Geoff Wright

Detailed Records

When I left school I applied for a job with the local electricity company (then called The Urban Electric Supply Co. Ltd) at 37 St Mary's Street and I worked for them until it was nationalized in 1948. It then became the East Midlands Electricity Board. I stayed there until I retired forty-six years later – with a break of four years when I was in the Royal Signals during the war.

My desk was on the first floor and overlooked St Mary's Street where I could see Hurn's the butchers and Muriel Hurn the dressmaker. At that time St Mary's Street was the main thoroughfare of the Great North Road and traffic was even worse than it is now in 1999.

Work in the electricity office was very

different in those days. All electricity accounts had to be calculated and written manually. I recall the domestic tariff was 12s per quarter and all units were threefarthings. The manager was Mr Wood and he kept a detailed record of consumers on supply. Bowman and Sons were the first to be connected to the supply in Stamford.

Electricity was generated in Wharf Road, now used as a depot. The supply was changed from DC to AC when Stamford was connected to the National Grid in 1937. At the beginning of the war the foreman was Jack Barnett but when I came back from the forces it was Bill Boyden. The records of the mains layout in the town were very inadequate and most of the locations of the town's mains were in the heads of Bill Boyden and his brother Bert!

Terence Asker

Barrows and Brooms

A purpose-built health centre was built in Wharf Road on a site where the town council stored their service equipment. There is an arch on St Mary's Hill with Business Link on one side and the town council on the other. That arch was the entrance to the council yard. In those days they had many, many employees. They would start off early in the morning with their barrows and brooms to go and sweep the footpaths. At that time Stamford was a borough and they were responsible for the town.

Sid Hall

'Queen Marys'

The greatest change in Stamford is the traffic. It used to be perfectly safe for children to walk and cycle to school. After the war it frequently came to a standstill and was often blocked for half an hour or more. I remember one well-known lady who was driving her car and when she was part of the way down St Mary's Hill, the traffic came to a stop. So she left her car where it was and went to do her shopping. Some of the vehicles going through the town were as long as St Mary's Street. They were low-loaders, known as Queen Marys. They were similar to RAF vehicles used for carrying an aircraft and sometimes they got stuck going around the sharp corner opposite Warunnee's Restaurant.

Stuart Rodgers

Fuelling the Boiler

On a Thursday we all went to Wharf Road to get the coke. All the children used to come with us. We took prams or barrows and sacking and we'd get six pennyworth of coke which was weighed out on large scales. If you were careful that was enough to fuel the kitchen boiler for a whole week.

Freda Clark

Blotched Legs

My brother would take the gardening truck and get coke for the fire which would eke out the coal.

If you sat too near the fire you got blotches on your legs.

Doris Borowik

Not a Lot

I went to Ketco Cement to work when they started in 1928 and I got 11d an hour. When I was married I was earning £4 2s 6d a week.

Dick Grimwood

Rented from Burghley

I worked part-time at the Arts Centre when they first started to make it into an arts centre. Before that, Burghley let out the Assembly Rooms and the other rooms. Then various people got together and rented it all from Burghley and it became an Arts Centre. I was asked to take on doing the bookings, looking after the building, opening it up at night for everything that was going on. I was supposed to be there for two hours in the morning but I was there for about ten – and I went back to lock up in the evening. I was paid – for my two hours! – and so were the cleaners but everyone else was voluntary. It was lovely in those days. That would be in the 1980s. I finished when the council took it over and they only employed people up to pensionable age so I had to leave.

We used to have a lot of dances and dinners. People in the choral society and the operatic society used to rehearse there. There was not nearly as much going on in the educational way as there is today. It was really for social events. We had jumble sales and what is now the theatre was then only a bare room. We had fun. Anna Timm used to do all the musical things and arrange the concerts. While I was there they were building the theatre.

Doreen Blackstone

Through the Shop

I was a book-keeper at Parrishe's. They were in Gothic House which was Wards before Parrishes bought it. I had to go through the shop and down some steps into an office down below. I worked with Cecil Parrish who was the brother of Bert, who used to stand outside talking to people. We had big ledgers. After the war, my husband joined the firm.

Mary Munton

CHAPTER 4
Winters

Harry Pond skates on Burghley Lake. The Marquess opened it to the public only when the ice was thick enough to skate on.

Extra Jumpers

In winter we froze! In the town we were not really affected but it was very slippy sometimes. We had a big house in St George's Square and there was no central heating. You just put on extra jumpers. We used to keep a big coat at the back of the drawing room to put on when we went into the hall! And we had long 'sausages' to put at the bottom of the doors to keep out the draughts.

Doreen Blackstone

A Peculiar System

Our shop was heated by a single radiator. There was a coal-fired boiler in the cellar which heated the whole building. Most mornings the fire had gone out and owing to the peculiar way the system worked, the hot water heated all the top rooms before it finally heated the shop. It would be eleven o'clock before there was any sign of heat coming through. It was very cold! I found a little oil heater which helped and I used to wear a sheepskin liberty bodice over my clothes.

The day the snow came down in 1947/48, a large low loader carrying a boat arrived in the town and parked at the bottom of Red Lion Square. The boat came up to the eaves of the buildings and it was there for six weeks. There was a rumour that there were 300 lorries marooned all around Stamford. It was bitterly cold. The streets were kept reasonably clear but it was incumbent upon a shopkeeper to clear his own shop front. Of course when you'd cleaned the snow away it was more

dangerous than if you'd left it on. So we then had to go and scatter ashes.

When we moved the shop into the High Street, I did this after the first snowfall and I had just finished cleaning it when a lorry went past and threw it all back on the pavement! After that I didn't bother any more except to put down some ashes. There is a little arcade down to the front of the shop and we used to put pieces of cardboard down to stop people slipping.

Stuart Rodgers

Blocked past Wittering

We used to travel out in two or three directions and one of those was in the Oundle direction. We used to have our lunch at the Red Lion in Warmington. We used to go out there fortnightly but for ten weeks in 1947 we couldn't get past Wittering. It wasn't so much the snow but the frost. We had a bit of sunshine and then it would freeze at night and there would be thick ice. Many lorries were stranded. It was reputed to be one of the worst places between London and Edinburgh. Up Casterton road the snow was lorry-high. I can see a sea of frozen snow all over what we thought was the road.

Frank Riley

Sledges

When we were quite young and growing up the winters were marvellous. We always had good snowfalls which fetched all the children

Gwen Clark on Burghley Lake in 1929.

out. We all had sledges and there was a steep hill in Lincoln Road which was excellent. Better still, there was little or no traffic. All the children played out together.

Pamela Clark

Tipping Ice in the River

They chopped the ice away in Maiden Lane, which was about the height of the kerb, to just below the King's Head. The rest they left. It was coming up to fair time and they had to clear Broad Street. They had lorry loads of ice and they took it down to Bath Row and tipped it into the river.

Frank Riley

Parked in Strange Places

In that bad weather of 1947, I was in the police force and I was on duty all day trying to find accommodation for the lorry drivers who had to leave their vehicles because they couldn't get any further. They just parked the vehicles anywhere and walked into town. We had to find blankets. When they went back to the lorries they found they had parked in very strange places. They couldn't see the road and one or two had parked on top of hedges.

Eunice Sorfleet

No Water

In 1963 we had another bad winter with zero temperatures. We had seven children and the water mains froze in the road. We were about three weeks without water. We were the last ones in the street to get any water back. The people at the King's Head, the Turners, said we could have water from them and I got it down to a fine art. I bought another bucket, which held one and a half gallons (I'd got a gallon one). In the morning I used to go across to the pub and fill both of them twice. That was five gallons in the morning and five in the evening. Of course, we had to use the water for everything. But at the end of the three weeks I was only going across to the King's Head once a day. In those days, Burghley Estates owned the water works.

Frank Riley

Skating down Broad Street

In 1962 I was at the TSB in Stamford and we'd take our skates in the mornings and we used to go straight from work. We'd go skating straight down to Wharf Road and we'd skate up and down the river under the Town Bridge. There was a very bad winter in 1940 during the war and I remember they never cleared the roads and I could skate down Broad Street. We were sledging down 'Rec hill' and Brazenose Lane.

Grahamme Sorfleet

Floods

When I was a child the ice used to be so thick on the Welland we used to take a sledge on it. I have seen floods come right up the 'Chains' which is where Warrenne Keep is now. There were people cut off and had to have boats to get them out. There used to be terrible floods until the water was restricted past Tinwell. It wasn't very good in 1941 when I got married which was on New Year's Day and a Wednesday. It snowed that day and it was around for six weeks but we didn't have so much drifting.

Maggie Graham

Keep Going!

In one of the bad winters I was living in the High Street and all the water froze. I was the only one that had water in the top end of the street. People used to come across with buckets. The Water Board said I should keep the water going. As long as I kept it going it wouldn't freeze. I used to leave the back door open and people just came in and helped themselves. You couldn't do that now!

Alice Burton

When the River Froze

The last time I skated under the bridge was in 1962. The river completely froze and the snow came over and you couldn't see the river. Peter Fancourt took his Mini down to the river and parked it in the middle.

Mark Hooson

Hard Enough to Skate

We used to skate at Burghley Park. Lord Exeter used to open the lake and there were notices put up in the town to say it was frozen hard enough to skate on.

Margie Harvey

A Lesson

I went out to the pub on a very snowy day and got detached from the rest of the group. I found myself in deep snow without my coat. It was in Burghley Park where the lake comes round at the top end and there is a slope towards the house. I really thought I was going to die. I remember it because it taught me quite a lesson – that you simply cannot give up. I was out for about half an hour or so.

Michael Tebbutt

Like a Wall

In 1947 we were snowed in. The traffic was all stopped on the Great North Road and you couldn't get into Stamford because it was cut off. I was living in rooms and I can remember on Barnack Road, the snow was high on the sides like a wall. Things were nearly at a standstill.

Maggie Graham

Boxing Day

That year it snowed on Boxing Day. It was quite a heavy fall. My father at the time was working at Allis Chalmers, the agricultural engineers and manufacturers at Essendine, and it was hard for him to get there. We had to get out and push the car, it was a big old Rover, that was taking my father into work from Ketton to Essendine up Tinwell Hill. I travelled with them into Stamford. It was not because there was that much snow on the road but it was slippy. That year there were a lot of severe frosts. And that damaged the wildlife. All the birds died.

Geoff Wright

Parsimonious

My father was a bit parsimonious when it came to the heating. It was very cold at home in winter.

Michael Tebbutt

Walked to Work

I remember when the A1 was cut off and there were a lot of people walking into the centre of town down the Casterton Road. That snow started in the middle of the afternoon. By six or seven o'clock at night there were quite a lot of areas cut off. Several of the Ketton lorry drivers were cut off in Derbyshire and stayed the night in remote farmhouses. I was working at the Cement Works at Ketton and I walked to Ketton the next morning. There was six to eight inches of snow on the road between Stamford and Ketton.

Geoff Wright

Off the Edge

You know where the road comes round behind Stamford School, where the Orion Arms used to be? Well, you could walk straight off the edge of the school field there. It's probably about sixteen feet high but there was a hard bank of snow. That was in the winter of '47.

Michael Tebbutt

CHAPTER 5
Leisure and Pleasure

An advertisement for Lowe, Son and Cobbold stout.

BOROUGH OF STAMFORD

Festival of Britain, 1951

ORDER OF THE

UNITED SERVICE

on

Sunday, June 17th, 1951

in

The Recreation Ground

at 8 p.m.

A service was held on the Recreation Ground to celebrate the Festival of Britain. The Revd Ernest Saunders, the Mayor's Chaplain and Rector of St George's, conducted the service. The Salvation Army Band led the singing and the addresses were given by the Revd J.P. Hoskins, Vice-Dean of Stamford and Rector of St Mary's, and the Revd R.O. Stubbs, Superintendent Methodist Minister. The Revd Charles Wells, Vicar of All Saints', led the prayers.

Dancing the Night Away

We used to go to dances at The Lansbury Club, in the Blackfriars Hall, which was Newage's social club. Blackstone's social club used to do dances and you used to get occasional dances at the Assembly Rooms. You would get a firm's annual dinner and dance held there. We did mostly jiving and the twist. Most of the lads used to prefer to smooch. It was the only way you got close to a girl.

Geoff Wright

Gala Occasions

From the Square

There used to be a grand Infirmary Ball held at the Assembly Rooms and all the people from the great halls and houses used to come to it. When I was sixteen my mother let us go into St George's Square to watch them arrive. There used to be a marquee across the square, almost from the church, and it went to the side entrance of the Assembly Rooms. The ladies wore beautiful ball gowns.

Maggie Graham

Grand Occasion

The Farmers' Ball was one of the grand occasions of the year and took place at the Assembly Rooms. When there were dances in the Assembly Rooms, the gallery used to be the supper room.

Margie Harvey

Beautiful Flowers

The balls in the Assembly Rooms were beautiful events. The Infirmary Ball was in aid of the hospital which in those days was called the Infirmary. That was the main event. One year Lord Exeter ran it and another year Lord Ancaster ran it. My father, George Blackstone, was always involved. There was a canopy outside the side door and you would go in and up some stairs which are no longer there to a cloakroom. Then you would come down the main staircase to the hall by the Blue Room into the Assembly Rooms. There were beautiful arrangements of flowers everywhere.

Doreen Blackstone

A Lot of Money

Many people would come from outside the town to the balls in the Assembly Rooms. I was working as a cellarman at Thomas's the wine merchants in Broad Street and I would go to the ball. The boss would give me £2 and Colonel Hart would reckon on me saving a table. The people who did the food were the Bartons in St Mary's Street. If people wanted wine, I would buy it with my £2 and then the customers would give me the money back. In those days a bottle of sherry or a bottle of port was only about twelve bob. But, let's face it, in those days it was a lot of money.

Dick Grimwood

A Pageant

They used to do a pageant in the Assembly Rooms every year and it was in aid of a children's charity. It was a very big occasion. People stood still and depicted scenes. One was *The Cries of London*. I can remember being in *The Water Babies*. I suppose they took the

TO CELEBRATE THE HONOUR CONFERRED ON OUR CHAIRMAN

SIR **PERCY LISTER**

THE ORGANISING COMMITTEE REQUEST THE PLEASURE OF THE COMPANY OF

Mr. S. Graham &
Mrs. Graham.

AT AN

ENTERTAINMENT AND **DANCE**

IN THE BLACKSTONE CLUB HALL,

ON FRIDAY, 17TH JANUARY, 1947

AT 7.30 P.M. 321

Ticket to an entertainment and dance in the Blackstone Club Hall, 1947.

The Bartons ran a bakery and confectionery business on the corner of St Mary's Street. They were also caterers for many of the dances and balls held at the Assembly Rooms.

The Infirmary Pageant parading along the High Street.

scenes from different books. It was a big thing in the town when I was young.

Doreen Blackstone

Taking the Bus

We used to go to the pictures on a Saturday night and later on we'd go to the dance. There were various dances around the town but the regular dance was the one at Bourne. They ran a good one there. There was a bus over and a bus back. They also had good dances at Wittering. In Stamford there were dances in the Drill Hall in St Peter's Street, and the Assembly Rooms. Johnny Dankworth and several named bands came.

Mick Warby

Dancing Schools

Wendy Lipscombe ran a school of dancing in the town. There was also the Vera Edwards School of Dancing which was in the back of the old Stag and Pheasant pub. That was in Broad Street and it is now a dental practice. She moved to the George Hotel tap which is now their conference centre.

Grahamme Sorfleet

Luverly Grub!

We used to cook potatoes in the oven, scrape them out, mix them with cheese and put a strip of streaky bacon on to and put them back to heat up again. They were lovely!

Freda Clark

Well Suited

Most of the lads would wear suits to go out – even when we went 'darting'. We used to get out to Oakham, Market Overton.

Geoff Wright

Fast Reporting

On a Saturday afternoon I used to go and see The Daniels (Stamford Town Football Club) play. They are still playing on Wothorpe Road. On the Saturday night I'd buy the football paper which came out almost as soon as the matches were finished. A van used to arrive in the square about seven o'clock in the evening and throw a bundle of papers out with the results in. We played snooker above Burton's in the High Street. It's now Clintons, the card shop. We went to a coffee bar in Red Lion Square where we could get espresso coffee. That's now Frangipanis.

Mick Warby

The Church Lads' Club

I belonged to the Church Lads' Club which was run by Miss Grace Lowe. It was kitted out with all kinds of activities – wrestling mats, boxing, fencing, ropes to climb, a reading room. This was in St Paul's Street. Wednesday nights were Club nights. On Sunday mornings we went to St Mary's church and in the afternoon we went to the Sunday school which Miss Lowe also ran.

Mick Warby

A Regular Treat

We went to the cinema twice a week on Mondays and

Trustees or supporters of the Church Lads' Club. Canon Day is on the left.

Thursdays. It was my father's main recreation. We paid about 1s 3d or 1s 6d. My favourite was *King, of the Kyber Rifles*. My father made a cat's whisker radio and I can see him now sitting in a bassinet chair with his headphones on listening to 2LO. He never missed the news.

Stuart Rodgers

The Picturedrome

The Oddfellows' Hall in those days was the Picturedrome and there were pictures outside of the film they were showing. Saturday afternoon was a children's matinée for 2d. You went through big double doors and there was a paybox on the left. A staircase led to the upper floor and on the walls there were pictures of film stars. The screen was on the wall and there was no curtain. The cinema eventually moved to the Exchange Hall in Broad Street.

The first Central Cinema was built in 1926 and the Picturedrome moved to the Corn Exchange in 1927. I believe it was one of the first public cinemas in this part of the country and dated from 1910 when it was first in All Saints Street. I remember the original Central Cinema being built. The old Blackstone's showroom was in Broad Street. It was impressive building with large windows, three at the top and three at the bottom. Blackstone's sold out to the Central Cinema Company from Cambridge and they kept the exterior and gutted the interior and built the cinema inside. It was very comfortable.

Ernest Warner

Barbara's Picture Palace

We used to go to Barbara's Picture Palace in Blackfriars Street on a Saturday afternoon. It was always well known and the place was full of youngsters and a man would walk down with a long stick keeping everyone in order. An organ played. One picture I remember in particular was a silent film. There was a railway line and a girl tied to it and the train was coming so we were sure she would be killed – but she wasn't. The Picturedrome was in All Saints Street. They took the Albion Hall and changed it into a picture house. Mr Dodman ran it.

Dick Grimwood

Regular Changes

When we were courting we used to live at the picture house! There'd be a film on Monday, Tuesday and Wednesday and then they would change it on Thursday, Friday and Saturday – unless it was something like *The Magnificent Seven* which would probably be on all week. Then on Sunday night you used to get a 'B' movie.

Geoff Wright

Long Serving Members

I first joined the Operatic Society in 1946, the first year after the war when it was re-formed. Now it is the Stamford Amateur Musical Society (SAMS). The first production we did was *The Rebel Maid*. My father was a member from

The Marquis of Exeter presents a silver spoon to Madeleine Young with Harry Warby (right) and George Essex (second right), among others, looking on.

1920. He did his last performance in 1947 when I did my first. They were performed in the early days at the Assembly Rooms and we moved to the Corn Exchange about 1927.

About 1926 there was a fire in the Corn Exchange during Fair Week. The fire brigade had to get through the fair. They went up the fascia of the building and, because it was spreading from near the stage, they had to fight it from both ends of the building. One of the firemen fell off the front of the building but because there was a fair stand below, it broke his fall and he got away with it!

They wanted to restore the place and they asked for subscriptions from organizations all round the town. A lot of organizations gave money to redo it as a theatre and a cinema. The Operatic Society gave money and they own shares in it. Nowadays, part of the lease states it is only rented out to tenants of the Antique Centre for forty-nine weeks of the year. The rest of the time it belongs to SAMS and, nowadays, the Pantomime Players.

Grahamme Sorfleet

The Dover Road

Herbert Parrish was an amateur clarinettist. They used to have plays in the Assembly Rooms performed sometimes by The Stamford Players who were largely a group of Stamford School masters and Stamford High School mistresses. I remember them producing *The Dover Road* and in the interval, music was rendered by Mr Harry Brook and his orchestra who were local musicians. Dances were also held in the

Assembly Rooms with music by Alfred Paine and his band. Alfred Paine came to Stamford to do the music at the Picturedrome which would be in the late 1920s. His boy, Eric Paine, was at school with me.

Ernest Warner

The Revellers

I used to run a concert party. We were called The Revellers and we started in 1951. We ran it to get some funds for the new school. My sister, Agnes Cooper, and I put our heads together and worked out how we could run this concert party. We got quite a good following and people used to ring up and ask us to go and entertain them. There was me and Agnes and Theresa, my other sister, Mr Charles and

Christine Charles, George Cooper, Jean Benns, Mr Brooks, Mrs Glenn and Mrs Brooks played the piano. Jill Cottrell was also in it and Jill and I used to sing The Nun's Chorus.

In one of the scenes from the show I was Britannia. My husband made me the shield with a Union Jack entwined and he made me the three-pronged trident. We borrowed a bulldog from Oates & Musson's shop in the High Street. Mr Brooks was dressed as John Bull and Betty Gregory and someone else, I can't remember who now, dressed as Irish women, then two others dressed in Scottish national costume and two were in Welsh dress.

I wanted to borrow my brother's fire brigade helmet but it was brass so Mr Grimes, who was the chief of the fire brigade at that time, lent me his which was silver.

Mr Rosser, when he was Mayor of

Sir Malcolm Sargent with the Gilbert and Sullivan Players, 1922.

Frank Hare (left) dressed for his role in *The Mikado*.

The Bowman family in the garden of their house in St Martin's. Margaret (left) was the secretary of the G&S Society.

Stamford, asked me if we would put on a show in the recreation ground in Coronation year – which we did, with the Blackstone's Follies.

Maggie Graham

G&S

When I was demobbed in 1949, I went and helped with *Aladdin* then and I've been involved ever since. My father was a big Gilbert and Sullivan man. When there was a breakaway group from the Operatic Society and other people in the town to form a Gilbert and Sullivan Society, my father took me along and a fellow called George Green, and Bill Ashton, and one or two others. We had several meetings at the Town Hall and formed

the Gilbert and Sullivan Society in 1950. The first production was *HMS Pinafore* in 1951. Harold Harvey, Mark Hooson, Eileen Fratton, Frank Norman, John Connell were all there. There was an arrangement then that the Operatic Society performed in the first full week after Easter and the G&S went on as soon as they had finished. We started rehearsals for that in October. We used to rehearse in the Albert Hall in the High Street any time we were not on the stage. That disappeared when Tesco's was built.

Grahamme Sorfleet

Secretary

My Aunt Margaret was the secretary of the Gilbert and Sullivan

Operatic Society and she roped in all the family. My father had a good tenor voice and he was in All Saints' choir.

Margaret Hare

Excerpts

I was in *A Rose without a Thorn* which was performed in the monastery garden at the George. Another time we put on excerpts of plays.

Jimmy Jackson

Early Days

The first production of the Stamford Shakespeare Company was in the Monastery Garden at The George. We used to sell soup during the interval. We had a big urn of soup which we used to wheel out to the audience and sell cartons at 6d each. The first production was *A Midsummer Night's Dream*. The first thing we had to do was erect a stand and a stage. It became very popular. Jean Harley and Mark Hooson asked me if I'd do the part of Bottom as I'd already done it but I was fed up with Shakespeare so I said no. I've always done front of house. Jean was a RADA student and she started the Company. We put on about seven productions at The George and then we went to Oundle in 1968 and used The Talbot for a year.

Grahamme Sorfleet

Founders

Jim Jackson was a member of St Martin's Players with me. There was Robin Cobbold, who has just died, and Charlie Fryer. The four of us were the beginning of the Shoestring Theatre.

Grahamme Sorfleet

SAMS to Shoestring

In 1944 I was in my first play. It was *The Farmer's Wife* and we put it on at the High School. Dorothea Till played the title role. In those days it was The Stamford Music and Drama Club and they put on an annual production. One year it would be at the High School and the next year it would be at the Boys' School. There was nowhere else to put on a performance in the town. Eventually we split and the drama side went one way and the music side another. We formed another drama society and called ourselves Stamford Amateur Stage. By that time the schools didn't want us performing in their halls. In Canon Day's time he used to welcome us. They eventually changed the name from Stamford Amateur Stage to the Shoestring Theatre. When the schools wouldn't have the Stamford Amateur Stage any more we went to the Darby and Joan club and performed there. Some plays we did at the Congregational Hall in Broad Street. We put on *Heartbreak House* there which was a Jean Harley production.

Jimmy Jackson

Hunting Green

When Lord Burghley was Master of the Hunt they used to wear green, not red, and would always meet in Broad Street on Boxing Day.

Doreen Blackstone

The Meet

When the Burghley Hunt used to meet on Boxing Day, the stirrup cup was served at the Lincolnshire Poacher by Peter Johnson.

Sid Hall

Fishing Match

At Blackstone's there used to be a fishing match and fishermen would be taken out to the River Nene at Tansor for the day by Wheatley's horse and cart. There were long seats in the cart and it was open when it was fine and covered if it was wet.

Dick Grimwood

Murky Water

They closed the swimming pool when there was an outbreak of scarlet fever. The water was so murky in that pool when I first came to Stamford that you couldn't see the bottom. Then they put a filter in it.

Eunice Sorfleet

Gypsy Meadows

When I was at Blackstone's we used to go down to Gypsy Meadows for swimming.

Jimmy Jackson

Cobbler's Hole

People learnt to swim in the river Welland. They used to go to the Engine Hole or Cobbler's Hole. There was a little paddling pool for young children. They used to hold the swimming galas there in the river.

Grahamme Sorfleet

Day Out

When we used to go to the swimming baths near the car park in Station Road, we went for the day and took our food. We even went off to do a bit of shopping and they let us back in.

Freda Clark

Stamford's Spa?

At the end of the second meadow, as we used to call it, in between Stamford and Tinwell, there was a round stone with an opening at the bottom where you could get spring water. We used to call it the Spa

Stamford Swimming Pool where so many children of the town learnt to swim.

Stamford Infirmary Fête, c. 1912. The parade is leaving the George Hotel through an entrance in Station Road which is now blocked.

because a lot of people in Stamford thought it was healing water.

Maggie Graham

Carnival Time!

There was once a Whit Monday Carnival which is now part of Stamford Festival. All the proceeds went to the hospital and we used to raise a lot of money. As a schoolboy at St Michael's, I was one of Robin Hood's men. We used to start in Broad Street and finish at Burghley Park. There was always a band, children and adults in fancy dress and people collected money as we paraded along the streets. We finished once at Barn Hill House.

Jimmy Jackson

Twinning

In September 1974 I was elected to the town council at a by-election. It was my first council meeting and a letter had come from France. They had written to the British Council asking which town would be suitable to twin with Vence. They were told that Stamford was the same sort of age and passed the letter on to our town clerk. The council turned down the idea saying it would cost too much money! The Mayor said that if anyone stated a twinning society the council might co-operate with them.

I went to see a man called Martin Jeffreys who was president of the chamber of trade that year and we both agreed it would be a great benefit to young people to start exchange visits. There was a Mr Johnson who had a business connection in Vence and he was interested in starting a society.

Later that year my husband and I were going to France and I asked the Mayor if he'd like me to speak to the Mayor of Vence. He thought it a good idea and I went and met Maire Maret, who was mayor, and some of the councillors. I had to make a speech about Stamford, in French, off the cuff. At the end of the speech they asked me what I though was the difference between Vence and Stamford. I replied: 'Vous avez le soleil!'. You have the sun. That was the headline in the paper the following morning!

Because Stamford hadn't replied to their letter Vence was going to cancel the request but I said: 'Oh no, I am here! I am a councillor from Stamford and I have come to arrange it!' And that was how we started. M. Maret came to Stamford and planted a tree, a metsequoia, on the meadows and this year the Twinning Association arranged to have a plaque beside it.

Soni Cloudesley Seddon

Cricket

We had a very good cricket team in Stamford which played in Burghley Park.

Sid Hall

STAMFORD INFIRMARY CARNIVAL

TICKET OF ADMISSION
for either

FETE IN INFIRMARY GROUNDS
on Saturday, May 27th

or

CARNIVAL BURGHLEY PARK
on Whit Monday, May 29th
PRICE 6d.

Nº 9207

Nº 9207

An admission ticket to the weekend of entertainment for the Infirmary Fête.

STAMFORD
VENCE

WHITSUN HOLIDAYS 26/31 MAY 8.

An early Twinning programme.

Bandstand

The town band used to play at the bandstand on the recreation ground.

Doreen Blackstone

Pageantry

There was often a pageant at Burghley Park and we would go and help.

Margaret Hare

Camping

When I belonged to the Scouts we used to go camping in a place called Shacklewell Hollow on the Empingham Road. We used to get a handcart filled with all the camping gear and pull it to the camp. The Scouters used to go in cars or on their bikes!

Mick Warby

Stamford Military Band in 1912.

You are invited to:

Lincoln Road Children's
Coronation Party

on Wednesday, June 3rd, 1953

at 4.30 p.m.

Children were invited to street parties to celebrate the coronation of Queen Elizabeth II.

Actors Robert Hardy and Rufus Sewell during the filming of *Middlemarch*.

CHAPTER 6
People and Places

Canon Day.

Edward Bowman (centre right) leads the parade through the town on 'Mayor's Sunday'.

Swinging Incense

In the early 1930s there used to be, every year, a service called The Church Workers' Festival. The choirboys used to meet at the Oddfellows' Hall and walk to one of the churches. We would go to a different church each year. There was a real kerfuffle one year because Father Bailey of St Mary's swung the incense.

Frank Riley

A Typical Country Parson

My father was a typical Victorian country parson and I feel I am just old enough to remember an era that you only find in books now. He was a curate at All Saints' church in 1896 and he lived until he was 97.

Mark Hooson

Mrs Tinkler

I went to Mrs Tinkler for music lessons at 32 Broad Street. You let yourself in the front door and the drawing room was on the left. That was used by Miss Wade who was a partner of Mrs Tinkler. If your lessons were with Miss Wade, you turned left, but if it was your day with Mrs Tinkler you went straight down the hall to the room at the end which I think she called the garden room. In those days I was scared stiff of

Mrs Tinkler! She was a gorgon to me but she was a first-rate teacher, there's no doubt about it. I'm very pleased I went to her. She used to tell me about Malcolm Sargent.

Ernest Warner

Mrs Tinkler

Mrs Tinkler was a petite, elf-like lady with dark hair pulled back. She lived in Broad Street in a double-fronted house almost opposite Traylen and Lenton.

Michael Tebbutt

Ninny

Charles Betts, Town Crier of Stamford.

Ninny Yates was one of the characters of Stamford. Everybody knew Ninny. He was a road sweeper. When I used to walk down to work, he'd be there in Red Lion Square and he'd say, 'Hey-up, Sorfleet!' I remember my boss saying, 'You don't speak to people like that, do you?'

Eunice Sorfleet

A Character

Ninny Yates was a character! He was a little eccentric but he was good-natured. I remember the crowd that cheered him on when he married his housekeeper at Barn Hill Methodist church.

Terence Asker

The Town Crier

You would hear the town crier any time. He would walk around the town and call out all sorts of notices. Now you only see him occasionally but he used to be around all the time. He made announcements so people knew what was going on. He always wore a long blue or grey coat.

Dick Grimwood

Colin Dexter

Colin Dexter's father had a garage. He was a small man with lovely rosy cheeks and he always wore a peaked cap. He was ever such a cheerful man. I worked in a fish shop then and I used to pass him as he stood at the door on my way delivering fish. He always had a word for everybody. I remember Colin as a boy when he used to go to the grammar school.

Maggie Graham

Only Taxi in Town

When I was a small boy I would come roaring down Empingham Road on my bicycle and Alf Dexter would be sitting in his armchair on a fine day outside his garage in Scotgate. He was the only taxi driver in the town. He took Margaret, my wife, to the hospital for the birth of both our children.

Jimmy Jackson

Alice Essex

Alice Essex was a big lady, rather fierce. She used to ride a high, 'sit up and beg' bicycle. I can remember her when I was working in the Arts Centre. She was involved there and I believe she organized everybody.

Doreen Blackstone

Mondoques

Alice Essex was a schoolteacher and she became very well known in the town because she used to do monologues. She would dress up in

Les Shaw escorts Jean Walker to the wedding of Barbara Wilcox and Clifford Truss at St George's church. Alf Dexter is in the background.

suitable clothes when she performed. She lived in Casterton Road.

Alice Burton

Silly Sammy

There was a man we used to call Silly Sammy, which seems rather hard. He was a very dapper little man who came from a very good family somewhere but who didn't wish to own him because he wasn't quite right in the head. He used to walk up and down the Wothorpe road because he loved trains and he liked to go and watch them. He

71

was always very well dressed.

Doreen Blackstone

Mr and Mrs Chambers

M r Chambers was the owner of Seccombe's and always dressed very smartly. He welcomed you into the shop. Mrs Chambers would put you behind a curtain while she brought out all these dresses for you to try.

Doreen Blackstone

Canon Day

W e used to call Canon Day 'Gaffer John' behind his back. When he retired he became vicar of St Martin's and a good friend. There was a company called the St Martin's Players formed and we did one farce a year. Canon Day made the Stamford School. He was the headmaster and when he arrived it was a very small school. He was the driving force and held in great esteem – and terror!

Jimmy Jackson

A Wonderful Day

F or many years we lived in a red-brick semi-detached house called Holly Bank in St Paul's Street at the top of Brazenose Lane. It now belongs to the School. In the other semi-detached house lived the Parrishes. Canon Day, who was quite a famous headmaster at the boys' school, and my father did a lot of church work together. They were both trustees of the Lads' Club which is now part of the school. Canon Day used to come along and see father before he

Margaret Hare sits on her father's knee. Her uncle, Hayden Hare (standing), became a well-known organist and worked with Sir Henry Wood at the Norwich Festival.

went to work in the morning. I always remember him saying 'Isn't it a wonderful day for Ascension morning?' It was quite a new idea for me. I had never thought of it like that.

Margaret Hare

Father West

In my grandmother's time, that would be about 1900, (she kept The Prince of Wales) they were doing some work by the old Priory and they came in at lunchtime and she heard them talking about digging up a coffin and it was something religious. They told her it was the body of Friar John. She went to Father West and told him and said he should go and claim the body, which he did. There was a procession from St Augustine's and Friar John was reburied in the cemetery.

Father, later Canon, West.

Canon West, from St Augustine's church, used to ride a horse to visit his parishioners in Stamford. He always had a pocket full of pennies to give to the children who used to run and open gates for him. He was an unusual figure in a big hat and breeches. He was so well liked that almost all of Stamford turned out for his funeral.

Maggie Graham

Malcolm Sargent

I remember Malcolm Sargent's mother and father. Harry Sargent was the coal merchant and if you met him anywhere he always had a joke for you, especially if you were a child. He was a very convivial man with a good circle of acquaintances. My uncle, Dr Hayden Hare, became organist at Great Yarmouth parish church. When he went there he began having music students who lived in the house and who were looked after by his wife. At some point, Harry Sargent wrote to my uncle and said would he consider having Malcolm as a student. He asked his wife and she said no because she'd like a little rest before she took in another anyone else. He suggested someone at Peterborough. Within a fortnight of Malcolm going to him, he wrote to my uncle and said, thank you for sending me a genius.

Margaret Hare

73

A young Malcolm Sargent with members of the operatic society.

Conducting

My dad played the cornet in the Stamford Town Band when Malcolm Sargent conducted it. Dad used to cycle in from Ketton with me on the front of the bike. There were buildings all along the eastern end of Bath Row. Dad used to come into band practice on a Sunday morning. The band room used to be behind the antique shop in St Mary's Hill. That shop used to be The Queen's Head. Behind that was a door into the yard and band practice room was in one of the barns at the back of the pub.

Buildings used to back on to the little mill stream bit where the railings are and the conker tree.

Geoff Wright

Hundreds of People

Malcolm Sargent lived opposite to my father when they were lads. I went to his funeral but you couldn't get in the church. I stood outside All Saints' and watched the people go in. There were hundreds of people there. There were lots of wreaths put all

74

around the outside of the church. One I remember was in the shape of a treble clef and in white carnations.

Alice Burton

Barriers

I went to Malcolm Sargent's funeral at All Saints' church. We couldn't get inside because there were so many people but my sister and I were close to the barriers. There were crowds and there were barriers all round the church. There were beautiful wreaths.

Maggie Graham

From Above

We were up in the offices of Phillips, Evans and Daltons and

ALL SAINTS CHURCH
STAMFORD

MALCOLM SARGENT
1895 - 1967

MONDAY, OCTOBER 9TH, 1967 AT 2.30 P.M.

Rector :
THE REVEREND CANON E. F. WRIGHT

The music for Sir Malcolm Sargent's funeral was provided by the choir of Peterborough Cathedral, whose master of music at the time was W. Stanley Vann. The organist was Barry Ferguson.

Sir Malcolm Sargent's grave in the cemetery.

watched Malcolm Sargent's funeral from there.

Glenda Parsley

Young Ginger

One of the stallholders at the market said that as long as he was in Stamford on a Friday, there would always be flowers on Malcolm Sargent's grave. When he [Malcolm Sargent] first died, the promenaders used to come on the anniversary. I can remember him when he used to play the organ in St John's church. He used to come to The Golden Fleece to get someone to pump the organ for him. Old Mr Sargent used to call me 'Young Ginger'! He used to work for Ellis & Everards, the coal people. The owner of the fish shop where I worked in Cheyne Lane, Mr Wade, used to get his coal from there and Mr Sargent used to come and collect the money.

Maggie Graham

Local Artist

Wilfred Wood was a wonderful artist in the town. He lived at Barnack but he did a lot of scenes of Stamford. He came into the shop one day and I said, 'why can I never find a print of your picture looking down St Mary's Hill?' He came back a few days later and said is this the one you meant? It was so he said he'd have it framed for me and he signed it, too.

Alice Burton

Official Photographer

Harry Burton, my husband's uncle, was born in the town. He was the official photographer at the opening of Tutankhamun's tomb with Lord Caernarvon and Howard Carter.

Alice Burton

Laurence Tebbutt

My father, Laurence Tebbutt, started off life as an architect, working in Traylen and Lenton's office in Broad Street. At the age of fifty-five he was totally fed up with architecture and decided he really wanted to have a second career. It was quite unusual in those days. He applied for a job as librarian in Stamford and was duly appointed.

After about five years he decided that the town needed a museum. He managed to persuade the town council this was a good idea and he set up a museum at the back of the library so he became the first museum curator. He wrote a number of books. The one that I think pleased him most was *Stamford Clocks and Watches* which was a provincial guide. I think he had about 500 printed by Dolby's. A whole lot of them went up in a fire and he lost about half of them. They are now changing hands at over £100 a copy.

He was quite a communicator and a lot of people were very fond of him. He had so many strings to his bow: he was an archaeologist, a sound recordist, a naturalist as well as an architect.

Michael Tebbutt

Stern

When I first joined the library Mr Tebbutt was in charge. He was very, very stern and you didn't laugh or muck about or even talk. The books we were after were Enid Blyton books which were like gold dust. If you'd got an Enid Blyton book you were lucky. Very rarely would you find one on the shelves.

Pamela Clark

On Television

Laurence Tebbutt came to see me one day and said he had the producer of Anglia Television, I think it was, who wanted him to go up into the tower of Peterborough Cathedral and explain the workings of the clock. He said, 'I don't know how it works and what's more, I don't know how I'd get into the tower of the cathedral so would you do it?' So I did! When I got there there were five clocks – a very old one, a modern one, one that was just part of a clock but it had an escapement or an interrupter gear and two others. It was winter so I had an overcoat and it was a very small room in which there was the producer, the cameraman, the script girl and two or three others. They had to use a fish eye lens.

Stuart Rodgers

One and One, Please!

Rene Beale fried fish and chips to order in the front room of her house

Laurence Tebbutt.

in Scotgate. They were marvellous. She fried only to order and she was helped by her friend who lived in the next house, Topsy Walker. You walked straight into the room through the front door and you could hardly see them for steam. You'd order 'one and one' for threepence, that is, one fish and one chips.

If you happened to be there at, I think it was half past eight in the evening, Rene would say to Topsy, 'It's time.' That meant Topsy got a jug and went into the White Swan next door to get it filled with beer.

Harold Harvey

Uniform

The old men at Browne's Hospital in Broad Street used to wear corduroy

77

trousers, velvet coats and top hats. That was the uniform they wore every Sunday when they went to All Saints' church where they sat in special pews. One had a parrot and I can remember him walking about the town with it on his shoulder.

Mark Hooson

Johnny

There was Johnny Aldwinckle, who was the son of a local farmer who walked all around the town all the time. He was part of the town.

Mark Hooson

Eric Clark and a friend singing in the choir of St Mary's church.

Choir and servers of St Mary's church at the annual supper in the Old Barn Restaurant in the late 1950s. Canon Hoskins presides.

Vincent Seccond

There was Seccond, the Italian ice cream maker who had a yellow cart and used to sell cornets to the children.

Mark Hooson

St Michael's Church

Grahamme Sorfleet and I were both choirboys at St Michael's. I joined St Michael's choir when I was seven and Ernest Warner, who was organist for thirty-seven years at St Martin's church, was my first organist and choirmaster at St Michael's, in his teens! I sang at his wedding. When he was away during the war we had a Miss Bettle who played the same voluntary before and after the service. I went back as organist at St Michael's church in 1952 and I was there for three years and there when it closed.

There was an interregnum and then we had a new parson who had come from Canada and he really didn't like the church and couldn't wait to open a similar church to the one he'd been used to in Canada. When he took over Christ Church, so St Michael's closed. I left just prior to its closure and transferred to All Saints'.

The first thing was the Church Commissioners said they would like the town to buy it for £90,000. The town spent two or three years discussing this and then they decided they hadn't got £90,000 and after another year or two the Church Commissioners said we'll give it to you! The town said, we haven't any money to do anything with it! That was when it was sold and turned into shops.

The church got into a terrible state. It was the responsibility of All Saints' church for a time and then it was transferred to St Mary's. In the days when it was All Saints', I occasionally borrowed the key and went in. I'd find somebody had left the tower door open and so the place was full of dead and decaying pigeons, and the bit of carpet was left rotting in the aisle, the old piano was still there, part of the organ had been removed and nobody seemed to want the responsibility of it.

It was an extraordinarily useful building because with chairs and its substantial gallery it would hold 1,100 people. It was the only building in the town that would hold that number.

I maintain that had the Assembly Rooms had not become available, St Michael's church might easily have become the Arts Centre.

Harold Harvey

Amusing

I was confirmed there at St Michael's church and I often find it amusing to go to the opticians or the building society – you can see where the pillars were. It is nice that Peter Fancourt keeps the clock going. It used to be both sides of the tower.

Mark Hooson

St Mary's Clock

St Mary's clock strikes ten at night and then it stops until seven the

St Mary's church fête in the 1950s. On the left is Mary Cook, on the far right is Mrs Hoskins. Looking over her shoulder is Gwen Clark and next to her is Isobel Clark.

next morning. That was done in 1927 when the manager of the then Stamford Hotel complained that the guests couldn't sleep because of the clock striking.

Mark Hooson

White Swan Passage

In White Swan Passage there were several slum houses, three or four facing each other.

Harold Harvey

St Mary's Street

The house where we live was a nursing home just before the war and the doctor lived in number 22 and owned the whole complex. It was also a maternity clinic. After the war, Williamson and Cliff bought it and then it was again sold to Neville Dilkes, the conductor. This end of St Mary's Street, from the church to Maiden Lane, was once full of doctors.

Margie Harvey

Straw on the Street

One of my early memories was of straw being put down on the street when a certain very well-liked and revered doctor was very ill and dying. He lived in St Mary's Street and they put the straw down to deaden the noise of the traffic.

Margaret Hare

The Midnight Baker

Askers used to have a bread round in the town. Vic Davis was the roundsman and he worked for us for fifty years. He used to work late into the evening and he got to be known in the town as 'The Midnight Baker'. He used to have a bread book and customers would pay him at the end of the week. Vic was very popular and when he died many of his customers turned up at the funeral.

Terence Asker

Rocking Boy

I played the guitar and was in a band called The Defenders. They called me Rocking-Boy Wright!

Geoff Wright

'Bread and Jam' Terrace

I came to live in Stamford just after the war in 1947. My husband, Eric, was a Stamford man and I met him when he was stationed at Castle Donington. We lived with my mother-in-law in Ryhall Road, in 'Bread and Jam' Terrace. It was called that because the people who lived there were paid so little they could only afford bread and jam to eat!

Freda Clark

British Legion

In the corner of the bus station used to be the British Legion. It was a single-storey prefabricated building. Torkington Gardens is where the original Cascelloid's factory stood and they had an extension factory where Somerfield's is. The antique shop opposite the town hall on St Mary's Hill was once the Queen's Head pub and the passage that runs down to Bath Row was called Queen's Head Passage.

Geoff Wright

Lill Clipsham

Lill Clipsham also worked for us for fifty years. Lill originally worked in the bakehouse but took over the sweet shop for us when my mother and father died.

Terence Asker

Grace Lowe

The Church Lads' Club was just a little further along St Paul's Street. There was a very good and devout lady called Grace Lowe and she founded it. It was with her money and a great deal of her time and attention that it was built and it remained as the Church Lads' Club for years. At some point the school bought it and it was turned into the art room.

Margaret Hare

Gerard Hoffnung

We had Gerard Hoffnung as one of our schoolmasters for a short time. He was just totally and utterly batty – a lovely, glorious eccentric! In comparison to the relatively staid, sober, normal type of master we had, it was quite a relief! He was always being 'wound up', which we did. I don't remember learning a single thing from him – but we had a lot of fun! He wasn't at the school for long, perhaps two terms. This was during the war. I think he had escaped from Germany and was working as a milkman in Hounslow before he came to Stamford School. He came as an art master although I don't think he had any qualifications. His Cambridge Union speeches are remembered by many people. You know, the man with the load of bricks and the letter about holiday accommodation 'a French widow in every room'. He was totally unknown when he came to Stamford.

Michael Tebbutt

The Surgery

The doctor's surgery was on the corner of Maiden Lane, right opposite the Arts Centre. It was in a large town house and the consulting rooms were just the rooms which hitherto had been either a bedroom, drawing room, dining room, etc. Dr Till was the principal doctor there. Dr Parry was also there.

Sid Hall

Bradshaws

Stan Bradshaw used to have his taxi rank and driving school in St Peter's Street.

Geoff Wright

Unlocked

Wheatley's was a garage opposite where we lived in Scotgate. I was told that at one time they had stabling for 200 horses. It later became a garage for cars. All the coaches and flies were left in an area behind Wheatley's which was called The Pit and they were left to rot. In the early 1940s, the tack rooms or harness rooms were all left complete and unlocked. Nobody wanted them. There were horse brasses and bridles hanging up and rotting.

Harold Harvey

Hire a Fly

The Pit is now Holden the builders' storage yard. Wheatleys was the place where you would go to hire a fly if you were going out to a dinner party or somewhere similar. Then it became full of lovely Rolls Royces when the motor car arrived.

Mark Hooson

Choirboys

My father was in the choir of St George's church for eighty-five years and I sang in the choir for thirty-nine years.

Frank Riley

The entrance to the cattle market, with Harry Pond (right) holding a book.

Harry Pond

Harry Pond was my grandfather. He started work as a clerk in Phillips, Evans and Dalton's and he left there and took a job as rate collector at the Town Hall. It used to amuse me because each year there would be a picture of the town council and they change every year. But there were always two people who never changed – one was the town clerk and one was the rate collector. He collected the money from the cattle market traders and from the people at the fair. In fair week he used to come home with a large rectangular biscuit tin full of goodies. He was also a great skater.

Stuart Rodgers

Dr Day

Dr Day was a big man with a big beard and he was a herbalist and I used to walk there from where I lived in Doughty Street. Where the North Street car park is now was once a thatched house and you went in and there were jars of this and that all over the place. He had a garden down on the Uffington Road. Some of the other gardeners complained to the council that it was getting overgrown with weeds. Dr Day invited the council to have a look at the garden and he explained the technical details of all the plants that he'd got and all the medical benefits.

Dick Grimwood

Inside the Stamford Institution.

A Gentleman's Club

The Stamford Institution, which is now the Language School on St Peter's Hill, has an interesting story. It took less than a year to build and I was talking one day to Dr Till about the Institution and I told him there was a family story which came from Valerie Mould that our great grandfather, whose name was Daniel Gilbert, and was a stonemason, built the Institution. Dr Till said he didn't think it was right because we have the name of the architect and the name of the contractor. I thought about this afterwards and realized that the contractor would contract out. Gilbert, at the time, was employing six men. Dr Till also told me that my great grandfather carved the lions on the bridge over Burghley Lake. Harry Pond was secretary to the Institution which was run as a gentleman's club. It had a library of over 8,000 volumes and a lady librarian. On the top was a camera obscura.

Stuart Rodgers

84

A function at Stamford Infirmary. Standing on the left is Canon Day with surgeon Mr De Bryn and seated third from the left is the Marquess of Exeter. The actual event has not been identified.

A mayoral procession led by the mace-bearer.

CHAPTER 7

Markets, Fairs and Festivals

A view of the Mid-Lent Fair in Broad Street.

The Mid-Lent Fair

The Mid-Lent Fair arrives in the town on Mothering Sunday and leaves the following Saturday. It has been a feature of town life since well before the charter of 1491 in which it is specified. It was once an important national event lasting for two or three weeks and during the fourteenth century attracted merchants to the town from all over the country.

Love it or Hate it

I love the fair! You either love it or hate it. I think it's wonderful! I always think of it as the end of winter. It has changed since I first knew it but from my bedroom window I can see all the lights and when the big wheel was in Broad Street near Browne's Hospital I could see it going round. I love the atmosphere of it and I always buy Grantham ginger bread.

Helen Grace

Everyone had a Go!

There was always great excitement in Fair Week. There was the Scenic Railway and the Whales and Peacocks. There were slow moving roundabouts. Everyone, whole families, would go on them. Grandma could always have a ride – she couldn't go on anything today!

Ernest Warner

Saved Up

There was one ride called The Whip which had cars which used to go round at different speeds. When I first started work I saved up to go to the fair. I had a good time, but I spent all my money and it taught me a lesson.

Mick Warby

Listening to the Steam Organs

The steam engines had big dynamos on them which produced the electricity to drive the rides. The fair used to arrive in the town on the Saturday night with their lovely steam organs and they used to give a concert. People used to crowd into Red Lion Square to listen. Then the engines went off to various places.

There was the Golden Galloper and The Cake Walk which I can remember coming ever since my youth. I believe it first came to the town in 1904. There were huge swing boats, the size of a single-decker bus. Columbia and Britannia, they were called. One had an American flag and the other the British flag.

Mark Hooson

Fire at the Fair

We were very, very busy at The Golden Fleece at fair times. The Cakewalk used to be right outside. It was there every year except for one when they brought what they called 'Over the Falls'. It was tarpaulin and boards. You sat on a step and they must have pulled a lever and you went sailing down a green 'carpet'.

That was the year they had a fire at The Millstone which adjoined The Golden Fleece at the back. They had some stables. There was a roast chestnut and fruit stall run by Hooton and Ett who came from Leicester. Apparently, one of them got a message to say that someone was ill so he went off and left the other one to put the fire out in the brazier and put it away in the stables. It couldn't have been right out. In the stables there was a little pony that belonged to a man we used to call Oxo Wood. He sold hot peas at the fair. This pony was in the stable and Mr Barker, who lived in a cottage next to the Burghley Arms and was the baker at the Co-op, used to get up very early and he heard the pony making a lot of noise. He investigated and saw the smoke so he got in touch with the fire brigade who were in Scotgate then. They woke us up and told us the stables were on fire. They were very worried because of the fair.

Maggie Graham

Fortune Tellers

The cakewalk was always near the Central Cinema and the Model Fish Bar. We used to have house parties for the fair. My brother was at Cambridge and he used to bring his friends. We used to buy sticks of Stamford rock and there were coconut shies. We'd win bowls of goldfish as prizes. There were a lot of fortune tellers.

Doreen Blackstone

An Odd Smell

There use to be a Freak Show which always had an odd smell. There was the fattest pig, and the world's largest rat. I can remember the thin man who shivered. We looked down on them.

Margie Harvey

Free Rides

There were the whales and the peacocks. You would sit in the head or the tail of the whales. They were a bit like gondolas. They were lovely. The organs were playing all the time. There were galloping horses which I liked. They were always outside our school and Pat Collins always finished putting them up by Monday lunchtime. When we came out of school, he used to give us all a free ride.

Maggie Graham

Challenge

There were boxing booths and you could go and challenge the boxers.

Mark Hooson

Cutting the 'Nugget'

In the fair week I used to have nugget in the shop and I used to buy it from a Mr Derbyshire who manufactured it. Once a year he use to come round. It used to be in round cakes, about twelve inches across and I used to buy about 70lb I had to cut it into pieces. I started off with a carving knife and my hand used to get ever so sore. I mentioned it to Mr Derbyshire and he said he'd get me a proper knife. He brought me one with a big blade and two wooden handles. It was steel but the sort that marks, not stainless steel. It cost me 25s, which was rather a lot in those days! Wherever you go in fair week there is nugget on sale. I don't know why it is so popular then. We also sold broken pieces of rock then which came in all colours. There was a lovely one that was red and a clove flavour.

Alice Burton

Soft

It's always called 'nugget' at the fair not, 'nougat'. It is a different thing altogether because 'nugget' is soft.

Stuart Rodgers

Cheap at the Price

A few coppers would give you an evening's entertainment at the fair. Holland's and Thurston's used to bring their big machinery into the town after midday on Sunday. People used to throw confetti and I've seen Horseshoe Lane covered. Thurston's put the dragons in Broad Street outside Browne's Hospital and it was put up on crates from Lowe's Brewery. There was an organ in the centre and waterfalls splashing into a 'lake' on the stage. Dancing girls would come on and do their routine ankle-deep in confetti.

Dick Grimwood

Hot Peas

We used to eat coconut chips, hot peas and roasted nuts and we had confetti and streamers. Vincent Seccond had an ice cream stand. The hot peas we sold on little dishes and you could put vinegar and salt on.

Maggie Graham

Hospital Benefits

On the Wednesday of Fair Week, the Red Cross ladies used to be on the cash boxes and all the money taken between two o'clock and four o'clock used to go to the hospital.

Maggie Graham

Steam Yachts

The steam yachts were always outside the Catholic church. My mother would say, 'You can go on it as long as you don't want me to come on with you!' I always went to the end so you got the biggest ride.

Alice Burton

Swingboats

There were two steam yachts. One was *Shamrock* and the other was *Columbia*. They were like big swingboats. The fair was in Broad Street, Red Lion Square and Sheepmarket; never on Bath Row.

Maggie Graham

A Ripping Time?

The first suit I bought was collarless with drainpipe trousers. I had a leather waistcoat as well. We'd been playing darts at Wing and come down to Stamford Fair. I had this new suit on and we went on the bumper cars. There was a bolt sticking out under the dashboard and it ripped a hole in the trousers. Part of the fair used to be where the bus station is now.

Geoff Wright

No Mess

They [the fair] might disrupt the town for a week and everybody moans but when they go on Sunday afternoon there is never any mess left. They are nice people, the fair people. I used to have them in. There was one stallholder who used to give prizes to children and she came for sweets and she never ever asked for a discount.

Alice Burton

Out of Bounds

The fair was out of bounds when I was at school but you were allowed to go with your parents. We used to go on Thursday afternoons which was closing day. My father would get 5s worth of coppers which would take us all round the fair. There were side shows and stalls. My favourite ride was the Caterpillar. You were supposed to go on this with your girlfriend. There was a cover that used to go over it and then there was a

draft which blew up and blew the girl's skirt up! The wonderful thing about the fair in the old days were the organs which played and had moving figures.

Stuart Rodgers

Grantham Ginger Biscuits

In fair week we always had Grantham Ginger Biscuits. We always had a penny to buy a bag of Sherbet and a piece of liquorice. There were also sugar mice.

Margaret Hare

A Few Years' Break

The fair didn't come during the war. Just a few things came onto the 'rec' and then before that there was a bit of fair on the car park which is the bus park now.

Doris Borowik

Win a Chicken!

One year a man came with a stall which caused quite a bit of excitement. He was called Chicken Joe. You bought a ticket and could win a chicken.

Maggie Graham

After Church

I don't think it is so strictly observed now but they were never allowed to come into the town until after the church services ended at twelve o'clock on Sunday.

Harold Harvey

A Fascinating Sight

I think the Fair is a fascinating sight because it is a mixture of the old and the new, mediaeval buildings and modern fair rides.

Mark Hooson

Official Opening

The Mayor began opening the fair in 1969.

Maggie Graham

St Simon and St Jude's Fair

The cattle and horse fair was another tradition of the town. The horses were always in Broad Street while the cattle were penned in High Street. The fair was discontinued, possibly at the end of 1929. An item in The Stamford Mercury in 1930 suggests the fair had moved to the new cattle market at the end of Station Road.

Help from the Boys

In November, for the cattle fair, the whole of Broad Street was divided up with pens and hurdles and the cattle were left standing around. Many little boys used to help move the cattle. I think there were two cattle fairs.

Ellis Miles

St Simon's and St Jude's Fair in Broad Street at the beginning of November.

Market day in Broad Street, probably before 1936. Browne's Hospital is on the left and the original Central Cinema building is on the right.

Straw Covered the Streets

At St Simon and St Jude's Fair, the cattle coming from Deeping, Tallington and all round there was brought into the town along the Uffington Road and into the Pinfold. That piece of ground from Pinfold Lane down to Priory Court was grass and the animals were put in there. Then the farmers would walk across the road to the Victoria public house. If you look at it you'll see over the front window are two hands holding two pint mugs which are touching each other. That is because it was originally called the Parting Pot.

All the High Street was always covered with straw, from the Co-op at the top right down into Red Lion Square. Each man who had cattle to sell brought them so far into the street and a man stood in between one lot and the next. Then at ten o'clock, the auctioneers and the men who were

buying started at Red Lion Square, walk right up and look at the cattle, making bids for what they wanted. They'd come up one side as far as the Co-op and then down the other side. This was in the High Street because the horses were in Broad Street.

It was November and so it was dark about four o'clock. So if you were down on the meadows or on Bath Row, you could see lights going up Easton Hill side. It would be one man with a hurricane lamp in front of the cattle and another man behind driving them home. There would be a trail of lights with the cattle in between.

Dick Grimwood

Boarded the Windows

When they had the St Simon and St Jude's Cattle Fair in November, they boarded up the shop windows because the cattle ran about the streets.

Margaret Hare

When the Bullock Took Flight

When I was at the Star Tea Store we had to screw planks across the windows to keep the animals out. We had an iron gate which we used to put up and customers would come in and close it behind them. On one particular occasion, someone left the gate open and in came a bullock. The manager was there and so was the man on the meat counter. I was at the end of the shop. The man on the meat counter got behind the bullock but it took fright and went to the bottom of the shop where there was a big rack of tins of biscuits on a slope with glass fronts. He left his visiting card all over those biscuits! We had to close the shop and clean everything.

Dick Grimwood

Small but Interesting

The Friday market was much smaller and in many ways was more interesting than it is now. There were not as many stalls and sometimes the contents of poor people's houses were laid out which the bailiffs had taken. People selling china would throw the plates in the air. There would be meat on sale and there was always a great crowd around to buy cheap meat. There used to be a great repartee between the market people and the townspeople.

Ellis Miles

A view of Stamford cattle market.

A decorated float at one of the Whit Monday Festivals.

Shouting

The market was very lively with much more shouting than today.

Sid Hall

Same People, Same Place

The same people would appear week after week at always be in the same place. Sometimes the stalls would be seasonal selling Christmas goods around November and December.

Helen Grace

The George Tap

All the farmers who came to the cattle market used to go into the George Hotel tap. It was the place to play darts, swear and tell stories.

Grahamme Sorfleet

Ice Cream Cart

The market was not as big as it is now. In the Arts Centre there was a Wilfred Wood painting of an ice cream cart which always stood at the top of Ironmonger Street. The cart belonged to Victor Seccond. As far as I can remember there were mainly cheese stalls and vegetable stalls.

Doreen Blackstone

Upside Down

During the 1939-45 war, the ice cream cart was to be seen upside down in a ditch on the Ingthorpe road opposite Tinwell Cottages!

E.C. Till

The Whit Monday Carnival

I was with the Congregational church and I knew Albert Cliff very well. I knew quite a few of the young people in the church and we decided we wanted to do something in the carnival parade so I went to him and asked to borrow a cart. He let me have one and he took it up to Halliday's yard for us which was just below the police station. It was a flat-topped cart and I went to some people in the town and got some thin but close-knit sacking. I took that back and laid it on the floor of the cart, watered it well and set grass on it. It made a nice lawn. Then we dressed youngsters as Indians and built a wigwam.

We went from Halliday's yard down to Red Lion Square where all the floats were collected up and then they started the parade. They went down St John's Street and along St Mary's Street, down over the bridge and up the hill to Barnack Road. Now, when the first float was entering Barnack Road the last one was just leaving Red Lion Square. Of course, horses were pulling the floats

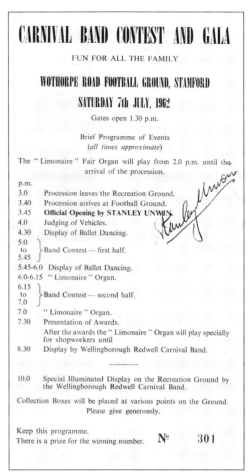

The Carnival Band Contest and Gala programme for 1962. It was opened officially by 'Professor' Stanley Unwin who signed the programme for Maggie Graham.

although a lot of the youngsters were pulling their own.

There were two bands, one in the front and one in the middle. It was a great day and it was very colourful.

Dick Grimwood

95

When the Lincolnshire Show took place in Burghley Park in 1950, Bowmans had a workshop there which showed their expertise and skills.

Lord Brabazon with the Marquess of Exeter (left) and Mr Mellerup of Blackstone's at the opening of the Industrial Exhibition on the meadows. The date is unknown.

CHAPTER 8

Shops and Shopkeepers

Crowds gather in Red Lion Square in front of Johnson the chemist and Pepper the butcher.

A.E. Smedley were butchers who regularly decorated their windows around Christmas with game. They described themselves as 'high class fish, game, poultry and venison dealers' and their shop was next door to the NatWest Bank.

Importance of Location

My father opened the jeweller's shop in Red Lion Square in 1939. It is now part of the Midland Bank. We had a large window which had a back closed in with little doors. Whenever we wanted something we had to open one of these doors and of course, had a good view of Red Lion Square. I used to start in the morning by washing the windows down and sweeping the pavements.

The shop belonged to the Midland Bank and they would never give us more than a year's lease. One day they decided they needed more space but they gave us eighteen months to find somewhere. At that time, in 1961, there wasn't an empty shop in the town but shortly we learned that a shop around the corner in the High Street, at that time Sketchley's Cleaners, was becoming vacant. I went to look at it and wondered how on earth I was going to manage in such a tiny place. But then I discovered it went almost back to the next street and was four or five times bigger than our present shop.

I was told we would do much better in the High Street and we did; we increased our business by 20 per cent in the first week. I began to hear people say they came down the High Street but they never went round the corner and they never crossed the square! It shows how important the location of a business is!

Above the shop was an office that was let to Kelham's the solicitors and then to Stevenson Smart, who were accountants and who are now part of Duncan Topliss.

Stuart Rodgers

Not Get Wet

You could walk from one end of Stamford High Street to the other in heavy, pouring rain and not get wet. Every shop had got blinds coming out over the pavement and a rope came from the blind down to the gutter with a big weight on the end to hold it in position. You could shop and remain perfectly dry.

Dick Grimwood

Harvey's Corner

Cumberland's the grocers was on the corner of Water Street opposite the George Hotel. They used to go out to all the villages. There was also the

Charles Rodgers with his wife Mabel.

Higgs the Confectioner became known as Harvey's Corner when the bakery took it over.

International and the Maypole which is now Stead and Simpsons. Parrish, the Outfitter, played in a local orchestra. He played the clarinet. He always stood outside his shop with a tape measure round his neck, talking to everyone. That is where Woolworths is. Gothic House, where Walkers is, was the ladies' department. Mr Harvey was the baker on the corner of All Saints' Place where Mandy's Flower Shop stands. That was known as Harvey's Corner. He had five sons.

Mark Hooson

Stamford Cough Medicine

When I left school and started work there was a chemist's shop which was the oldest but one chemist in the whole of England. They sold Stamford Cough Medicine and Mandle's Paint for mouth ulcers. They made it themselves and it was wonderful stuff.

Farndells had a chemist's shop in St Mary's Street. Next door, where Jeunesse is now, was Grimes the ironmonger. When you went to buy something off Sid Grimes he did his best not to sell it to you! I remember going into his shop once for some twelve-inch brackets for a shelf. 'No', he said, 'they're too big.' So I said, 'But I want some, Mr Grimes.' 'No', he said, 'You'll put a lot of your heavy clocks on and they won't stand it. I should have ten-inch if I were you.' He was like that with everybody.

I once went to get some copper wire, thick stuff. He pulled a paper package off the top shelf (with about an inch of dust on it) and it had a label inside and I think the date was 1899. What on earth was it like when he had to take stock?

Stuart Rodgers

Every Sort of Smith

I was born in Broad Street. My grandmother kept the grocer's shop and my grandfather, Samuel John Sorfleet, was a blacksmith, a whitesmith, a silversmith – every sort of smith. He had two workshops, one where Sycamore's Garage is now. There used to be all little workshops there. He had another in East Street which was taken over by Stamford School in 1954/55.

When my father and his brother took over the shop after my grandmother died, and became household furnishers, carpenters, upholsterers, cabinet makers, french polishers. They split up about 1926 and my father kept the shop. It only closed during the war because my father was on the reserve. He had served in the First World War in the RFC. He was called up six months before the war started.

Grahamme Sorfleet

Always a Chair

If you had a child's ration book, sometimes you got a banana. I always went to Eayrs, the grocers. It was a lovely family grocers and that was at 8, High Street. And there was always a little something under the counter. The assistants were so nice and nothing was too much trouble. There was always a chair for you to sit on and the assistants wrote down what you wanted in a book. Then when you got

Samuel John Sorfleet outside his workshop in East Street. Note that he dealt with 'Hot Water Apparatus' among other things.

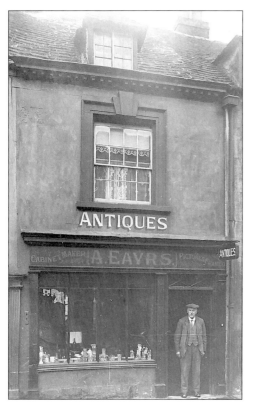

Arthur Eayrs standing outside his antique shop.

your groceries, you went and paid. Mr Ingram used to bring the groceries.

Freda Clark

Down the Side

The Edinburghs used to have an antique shop in St Mary's Street where the saddlers is now. Major Edinburgh's brother, Eddie, and his mother lived next to us in Broad Street which is now Petra. You went down the side and there was a house at the back and the shop was at the front. Behind that there was a bakery and you went down the passage to the Crown and Anchor pub. In those days you could go through the Crown and Anchor to get into the High Street from Broad Street.

Grahamme Sorfleet

Sugar Bags

You would get cards in with the tea and Richard, my brother, and I used to collect them. Mr Ingram would take the duplicate cards from each place he went and then swap them for those we hadn't got.

Miss Pridmore used to tie up bags of coffee and sugar. The coffee bag was red and the sugar bag was blue. They used to shake them and bang them on to the counter to make it settle.

In Riley's shop in Maiden Lane, they used to pull down an orange blind when it was sunny.

Pamela Clark

Photographers

Charlie Kemp and his stepbrother, Paul Brand, used to be the local photographers before Hinsons.

Grahamme Sorfleet

A Pennyworth of Broken Biscuits

My mother had her groceries from T. & J. Eayrs' in the High Street. They delivered to Melbourne Road on a Wednesday afternoon. So I would run from the Bluecoat School to Eayrs' shop and I'd get a ride home! T. & J. Eayrs' eventually became the International

Stores. My mother would buy sausages from Morley's at the end of Water Street. Morley's was on the end of the Anchor Hotel. Cumberland's was opposite The George. I would go in there and get a pennyworth of broken biscuits, and sometimes there would be part of a cream biscuit!

Ernest Warner

Free Delivery

Cumberland's were *the* grocers. They were on the corner of Water Street and High Street, St Martin's, and someone would come to your house to take your order. They came out to all the villages.

Margie Harvey

Wonderful Service

These well-known firms would look after their customers wonderfully. There was a greengrocer who was at the bottom of St Paul's Street and they would send someone to the house every day for an order. The butcher also came up to the house. There were two very good grocers that we loved: one was Young's which was in St John's Street and the other was Eayrs' which was at the bottom of High Street. They had lovely big tins of biscuits and you would choose what you liked and they would weigh you half a pound or whatever you wanted. That would be delivered and you would pay at the end of the week.

Margaret Hare

Hair Restorer

In Red Lion Square was Johnson the chemists. Mr Johnson had a big sign inside his chemist shop which was over the counter. It read 'Johnson's Hair Restorer'. And Mr Johnson was as bald as a badger!

Dick Grimwood

Penny-farthing

My grandfather started up in business in Oakham and my uncle had an umbrella shop in Stamford. My father was a tailor and first worked for Richard Bell in Scotgate in 1892. He started in business for himself at 69 High Street where his brother had a shop. He did tailoring upstairs. He was a journeyman and he had a bike, a penny-farthing, which he used to ride. He moved to the shop at the top of Maiden Lane in 1805, numbers 2 and 3. There were eight bedrooms.

When I left school I went to learn my trade at a big store in Nottingham. In the first year you always had to serve in haberdashery. I joined my father when I was demobbed from the war in 1946 but there was not so much call for haberdashery then. We kept needles and pins and lead weights. There was a passageway between number 2 and number 3 and when I married I moved into number 3.

We were linen drapers and sold sheets, pillow cases, bolster cases and blankets. There were only natural fibres in those days. People had feather beds which we didn't sell but we were always asked for 'bed covers' which were for putting the feather beds in. They were made from unbleached calico or twill. This was before the days of interior sprung mattresses. We sold men's outfitting and would measure men for new suits. We bought our stock from wholesalers in London, Nottingham, Huddersfield or even Peterborough.

My father was a credit draper and he would do the rounds of the villages to collect the money. He gave up driving when he was eighty-three.

Frank Riley

Making a Profit

When we moved to the shop in the High Street, I had it on a lease and eventually the property came up for sale – with ninety-one others all around the country. It belonged to a charity and it was on a thirty-five year lease at £7 a week. That was unbelievably cheap because today it would be nearer £400. It is a big shop and there was a flat over it and there was a little shop next door. We had been paying £1 a week rent in Red Lion Square but when we had the rent from the other shop and the rent from the flat, we made £1 a week profit.

Stuart Rodgers

Bulldogs

Oates & Musson's was where Dorothy Perkins and Burtons are now. They had two bulldogs. They looked very real and one had a chain around its neck. If you pulled it the dog

growled. As children we were fascinated by those dogs.

Pamela Clark

Changes

There was a shop owned by Oates and Musson who were antique dealers. They were furnishers, really, but there was an antique department in the crypt below the shop. Scotney, who were antique dealers on St Mary's Hill, had a crypt below their shop. It's now an Italian restaurant. There is a lovely little shop opposite Lloyds Bank with bow-fronted windows. It used to be the Belfast Linen shop before they closed it this year. I can remember it when it was a jeweller's shop.

Mark Hooson

Changes

Mr Everard had a jewellers next to Freeman, Hardy and Willis. Pinney's were in the square. The Red Lion Café became Finlay's shoe shop before it was taken over by Clark's.

Maggie Graham

From Cheese to Cloth

Where Paul Richmond is was a cheese shop and then it became a ladies' needlework shop.

Phyllis Hall

The top of Ironmonger Street, showing The Vaults public house.

Changes in Ownership

Fancourts used to keep the garage that then became Marshall's in St Paul's Street.

Frank Riley

Piled on the Pavement

There was a man who used to sell Stilton cheese in High Street St Martin's. He used to have the cheeses piled up outside on the pavement. My grandfather used to buy a half Stilton at Christmas.

Stuart Rodgers

Candles

In Oates & Musson's there were two bulldogs they used to have on show in their windows. When you pulled the leads they used to bark!

They used to make candles in Elm Street when my mother was a girl. Mr Cade had the confectionery shop at the beginning of St Paul's Street before it was Marshall's. Middleton's, a men's outfitters, was next door and between them was a side entrance. Mr Middleton had a housekeeper.

Maggie Graham

Pots and Pans

Jeunesse in St Mary's Street was once Grimes the ironmonger. He hung all his galvanized pots and pans outside. Everything spilled out onto the pavement. Fancourt's, the pork butchers, is a long established firm. Stamford is unique in having three or four fine pork butchers which attracted people from many parts of the country.

Mark Hooson

Next to the Post Office

Bassendine's was a shop I remember often visiting. There was the post office, then the pork shop and then Bassendine's.

Freda Clark

Very Cheap

In the High Street before Woolworths, there was something called a penny store. It was a 'walk in' with counters each side and you could buy things very, very cheaply.

Margaret Hare

T. Woods

I had a sweet shop, called T. Woods which was my father's name, and which was next door to the Sugar Bowl in the High Street. I sold anything from jar sweets to all the better chocolates. I sold bull's eyes and humbugs. I often think back to the time I had about twenty-five different reps come to see me to sell me sweets. I had a children's counter and sold sherbet dips and sherbet fountains, dolly mixtures and jelly babies – anything that you could sell two for a halfpenny.

When I left school they really didn't know what to do with me so that was why my father bought the shop. I could be there but also look after my mother if she needed me. That was in 1932 and I sold it in 1974 after my father died. I sold it to the present owners who had the Sugar Bowl which had been next door only for a year. Before that it was a gents'

hairdressers and owned by Jim Lambert. He did hair at the back and there was a tobacconist's at the front. Mr and Mrs Baum bought my shop and made it into a take-away attached to the Sugar Bowl – and we have been friends ever since!

Alice Burton

Sweets in Broad Street

I was born in Cemetery Road which is now Radcliffe Road and we moved when I was little to The Vaults pub at the top of Ironmonger Street. There used to be a needlework shop there but now it's an estate agent's. Then we moved to The Star and Garter in Scotgate where we lived until 1939 when we moved into Broad Street to the sweet shop One side of us was Sorfleet's and the other side was Edinburgh's, the antique shop.

My parents bought the shop in Broad Street with the idea that it would be something for me to carry on doing. I used to help in the shop a lot when my mother had an operation. I was off school for a long time and then they came and fetched me back even though I was fourteen and I was only allowed to work there for about an hour after school. Mrs Sorfleet, Grahamme's mother, came and managed the shop for a while. We used to sell soap flakes, dummies, Beecham's pills and all sorts of other things people needed as well as sweets and chocolate.

Doris Borowik

The Star and Garter in Broad Street.

The Best and the Worst

The worst thing that happened was the pulling down of some fine buildings at the top of the High Street. The Albert Hall stood where Tesco's is now. The place that is Wilko's was an outfitter's shop and they have kept the big, glass dome inside. Westgate House was a very nice building until it was covered with that speckled plastic.

On certain days, when the brewery in Scotgate were draining the vats of the hot water they sloshed over the barley, the drains outside the post office used to steam! There were wonderful smells of mashed barley! It was smells that one remembers.

Mark Hooson

Differences

One principal difference between Stamford now and Stamford thirty years ago is that you would have great difficulty in finding something to eat after six o'clock at night. Apart from the fish and chip shops and the hotels there was nothing, certainly nothing like you have now.

Sid Hall

Only One Shop

When I first moved to Masterton Road there were only four houses and we were surrounded by meadows. There was only one shop – the Co-op in Doughty Street – but later the Drift Stores opened and Mrs Smith had a little general store built on the end of her garden. It's now a fish and chip shop.

Maggie Graham

'Wheezo' Bones

Where the Chinese takeaway is there used to be a newsagent's and

Eliza Sorfleet ran the family business in Broad Street. It is now the Congregational Hall.

This row of buildings in High Street was demolished to make way for a Tesco supermarket.

next to that was 'Wheezo' Bones' fish and chip shop. Round the corner from Hindmarsh's was a butcher and past the White Swan there was a man called Simpson who used to have a cycle shop. It was an Aladdin's cave! Fred Wade used to have a scrapyard at the beginning of North Street and the printer's was Day and Plant's carpenters shop. They bought it off Fred Wade. Randle used to run a carpet shop near there.

We used to meet up with mates on a Friday dinner time and have fish and chips. It was either at Albie Glover's at the bottom of North Street (it was really called Frisby's then) or at the Model Fish Bar in Broad Street.

Geoff Wright

Ladies at the Front

My husband, Bazyli (we all call him Basil), started the barber's shop in St Paul's Street in 1959. He used to work at the gents' and ladies' hairdressers in the High Street where Chez Soi is now. The ladies' was at the front of the shop and the gents' was at the back.

Doris Borowik

Hang Out Your Wares!

On St Mary's Street there was a butcher, Bland's, which was almost opposite to Fancourt's where Georgi is now. You would go by there and see a whole carcass hanging over the pavement.

Sid Hall

Taken Away

There was a butcher's shop in the High Street where the MIND charity shop is now and called Adams. And there was an interesting butcher's shop in the middle of the High Street called Grant's. This was pulled down when Woolworths came in the 1940s, and the whole building was taken to York where it was re-erected.

Ellis Miles

Smart

Next to Seccombe's, which was a smart dress shop where John Sinclair's is now, was Kelham's mini-market and next to that was a shop selling nice children's clothes.

Phyllis Hall

Roasting Beans

There was a lovely old shop in Ironmonger Street – Bowman & Essex. They used to have bacon hanging up and they'd cut a piece off for you. They roasted their own coffee beans and the smell…!

Alice Burton

Bargains!

After Mr Hayes, who had the shop next to the Sugar Bowl, there was Mr Bontoft who sold bargains. He used to go up to London and buy sheets that had been all piled up and the edges were marked. They were perfectly all right and the first time they were boiled the marks came off. He used to sell these really cheaply. And he sold corsets.

People wore corsets in those days, and liberty bodices to keep you warm. When I was thirteen and I 'blossomed out' my mother had to get me kitted out. There was a Mrs Boyden – Boydens were coal merchants – who lived in St Peter's Street, and she was a Spirella agent. My mother carted me there and I had Spirella corsets and Spirella bras which made me go like a round tower! They cost 25s which was a lot of money then.

Alice Burton

Family Business

My father was Augustus Asker and my brother Ray took over the bakery business from him when he retired. When Ray retired, Stuart, his son, took over. Kerry, Stuart's son, works in the bakehouse. In 1947 when I left the forces, I helped with the accountancy side which I still do.

Where I live in Broad Street there were originally two shops. One was run by Frank Newbon who was a cobbler and the other was our baker's shop and sweet shop before we moved it into Red Lion Street just down the road. The Broad Street shop then became a sweet shop only. All the Asker family lived at 51 Broad Street at one time. We all worked in the bakery business. When I was a lad I always delivered bread on a Saturday and that was my pocket money.

Terence Asker

Those were the Days!

The Misses Musson were two sisters who kept a sweet shop in Maiden Lane and then they moved to the top of Ironmonger Street.

Ellis Miles

Before Supermarkets

Peatling and Cauldron were wine merchants in the town. Wine Rack occupy their premises now. There was a mini-market which was operated by a family named Parker which was in the High Street near the library. This was before the supermarkets came to the town.

Sid Hall

Service

We would come into town shopping and go to the fish shop. It is now incorporated into Westgate House. I can remember so well, they came out and served you in your car! You didn't have to get out! Parrishes and the International Stores in St John's Street had similar methods of payment to the Co-op.

Mark Hooson

The Bombay Brasserie

Where the double glazing shop is now, next to The Bombay Brasserie, it used to be Mr Boon's garage and he used to have petrol pumps on the front. The Bombay Brasserie used to be Flander's Flower Shop.

Geoff Wright

Scrounging Coupons

We didn't marry until 1948 which was after the war but to get my things ready for the wedding I had to scrounge clothing coupons to buy a dress. I went up to Mr Hudson, whose bakery was where the Bay Tree tea rooms is now, and asked if they could make me a cake. They said they would willingly make it but I'd have to provide my own fruit. So I was scrounging from customers to get two ounces.

Alice Burton

Buy Now, Pay Later

We had just moved to Lincoln Road and the baker came. That was Mr Marshall. He used to come any old time of the day. You didn't pay then, you paid at the end of the week. Mr Bone delivered fish on a bicycle and Mr Bee would come with a bucket and a measure to deliver milk. We always had a jug ready to put it in.

Freda Clark

Long Established

As far as we know, there has been a bakehouse in King's Mill Lane for 200 years. Augustus Asker took it over in 1928 when he left Hudson's, the bakers in St Paul's Street. He used to insist on making the dough by kneading it by hand it in a big trough. It was very hard doing it this way and it took a long time for Ray to persuade him to get a dough machine. When Ray took over the business, he developed the fancy cake and pie side and also built up the wholesale business. There were many bakers in the town years ago including Harvey's, Marshall's, Foreman's, Hudson's, Tyler's and Hill's. Tyler's were where Cantrell's bakery was in St Paul's Street until recently.

Terence Asker

Outside Catering

The Central Café was in the family for about sixty-five years. Mr Henshaw, who was a baker, used to own it before our family had it. My husband's father and sister were in partnership and it was called Neve and Parsley first. Then they went there separate ways and Neve had a café in the High Street. My husband, Derek, then joined his father. They did a lot of outside catering – sometimes six weddings on a Saturday. We did catering for Burghley House.

It was a very interesting café. We were well known for our steak and kidney pie, the real old-fashioned doughnuts and our mince pies. People came to us for meals and we were always open on Sundays for roast beef and Yorkshire pudding. Baked jam roll was another favourite. People came from all over. Different stars came in – Cliff Richard used to come quite a bit in the Sixties. Roy Orbison came in once and so did Lenny Henry, Gene

The Central Café in 1936.

People used to queue right out of the door. We were always busy. The Central Café was a meeting place. We used to do lots of afternoon teas.

Glenda Parsley

First Supermarket

There was a church hall called the Albert Hall where Tesco is now and it had a quaint arched door. I think Tesco was the first supermarket in this area. The funds raised from selling this went to build the United Reformed church hall (which was then the Congregational church) round the corner in Broad Street.

Sid Hall

Spotless

Jim Pepper had a butcher's shop in Red Lion Square. You climbed up two steps to go inside where it was spotless. The butcher was there with his block and all the meat hung round the room. There were steel racks going around the inside and suspended from hooks were knives, sharpeners, and cleavers – everything a butcher needed for his trade. In the corner was Miss Pepper. She died recently aged 102. You told her what you wanted and she conveyed that to the butcher, and she always took the money. Miss Pepper was dressed in immaculate black clothes and she wore a black blouse with fancy work all round the neck and an absolutely perfectly white apron.

Dick Grimwood

Pitney, Lesley Crowther, Edmund Hockridge, Duncan Norville and Henry McGee.

We had a coat of armour on the stairs which used to interest a lot of people. Children used to love it. We didn't know who it once belonged to. The bakery was underground, beneath the shop. Gordon Berridge was our baker and he used to go in about five o'clock in the morning. Derek used to go in about nine but if the baker was off he used to do his work. We did take-away food. People used to order buffets for parties.

We catered for large dinners too, often for up to six hundred people. Then we used outside help. We used to cook the turkeys and hams in the big baker's ovens. When we did away with the catering we started a take-away service of lasagne, liver, bacon and onion hotpot and things like that. We cooked joints of beef and pork and cut slices for rolls.

Out of the Window

Mould's shop was at the bottom of St Mary's Hill. Robert Mould was married to my aunt, Florence and he ran the shop as a draper. They sold everything. The shop has been several different businesses and at one point when Robert Mould had it, it was burnt down. A fire started and their baby, Leslie, had to be dropped out of the window into the arms of a waiting fireman. I think it happened in about 1914.

Stuart Rodgers

The Central Café's famous suit of armour.

Drapers and milliners, Mould's shop on St Mary's Hill sold everything a housewife might need.

CHAPTER 9
Wartime

Military parade along the High Street, 1945/46. Mary Goddard, on the left with the bicycle, looks on as they march towards Red Lion Square.

Stamford was not greatly affected by the war except for a substantial influx of Polish, Italian and American troops who were stationed close by.

A Reserved Occupation

If you worked at Blackstone's during the war it, was considered a 'reserved occupation' and you weren't called up. If you went to enlist then you were sent back and told they'd send for you if they needed you. You had to do something extra and I was in the Home Guard; that meant you could be on all-night guards, watching the railway tunnel or something like that. Then you would still be at work the next day.

Jimmy Jackson

Gas Masks

I remember being issued with a gas mask. The teacher said we were going to have a practice, putting the gas mask on and running across the lawn to where the shelter was. You couldn't breathe properly. They were Mickey Mouse faces.

There was a line of bombs dropped near Stamford but only one went off and that was close to where we lived. The first one dropped somewhere in Drift Road, one in the Avenue, one at the back of our house where there was some waste ground and one on Rutland Road. I remember getting up in the morning and looking at the coal-house door which was completely caved in.

After the war our road had a party. There were two parties, for VE Day and VJ Day. For VE Day we had a street party and I think for VJ Day we used the Guide hut in Conduit Road. There were a lot of kids down our way. We lived in a block of four, on the end. There were four of us, five next door, six in the next house and two on the other end.

Mick Warby

Tear Gas

Everybody had gas masks and we had to carry them wherever we went. My father used to test them. He would go to the villages and take tear gas and blankets with him. Then he'd go to the village hall, hang up the blankets and put the gas canister inside. Then all the villagers had to put on their gas masks and walk through the hall to make sure they were all right. Then he'd roll up the blankets and put them back in his car. Sometimes we'd go with him and when we got home we were all streaming!

Eunice Sorfleet

The gas masks were horrible. They were like big trumpets with a rubber part which fitted over your face. There were holes in the front which I suppose would filter out all the gas.

Maggie Graham

Wet! Wet! Wet!

My mum had to learn how to use the stirrup pump. She went to the

From left to right, Stuart Rodgers, Bill Nash and Charles Kemp the photographer in their Home Guard uniforms during the Second World War.

police station and all the police wives were there. They switched the water on and my mother had pointed it in th wrong direction and drenched the next-door neighbour!

Eunice Sorfleet

Too Young

During the war they were calling for special constables so a friend and I went down to the Town Hall to volunteer. They didn't know anything about it. So we went up to the police station and asked if we could be special constables there. They said we were too young so after that we said when they want us they can come and fetch us! So

we went and joined the Home Guard and we were there for about six months before we went into the RAF.

Stuart Rodgers

Car Bombs?

My father was a police sergeant at Stamford police station. When the war broke out he was due to retire so he was made Bomb Reconnaissance Officer for this area. He looked after the special constables. He used to go to all the villages and people would hand him unexploded incendiary bombs and anti-personnel bombs. He used to put them in the back of his car, which was a Hillman Minx and drive off to Wittering to get them defused. He got quite a reputation at Wittering! They used to say, here he comes again – and dive under the table!

Eunice Sorfleet

The Cornstall Buildings Bomb

One Thursday, a German aircraft flew across the town, machine-gunned and then dropped a bomb – which didn't go off. The bomb went through the side of a house in Cornstall Buildings, St Leonard's Street, where a lady was sitting on a settee with her baby. It pushed the settee aside and the side of the house fell in. Her husband came back shortly and got them out.

Stuart Rodgers

Tea Time

It was a Sunday afternoon and I believe they were having tea when the bomb sailed through the house. My parents put up Captain Green who defused the bomb. My father, Sergeant Stiff, was there.

Eunice Sorfleet

Sergeant Stiff (right) with one of the larger unexploded bombs to fall in Lincolnshire. This one, too big to get in his car, fell in the garden of 45 Drift Avenue in 1942. It is not the one which fell on Cornstall Buildings as is often quoted.

Food Shortage

We were in Wales when war was declared and came scurrying back to Stamford as everybody did. Everybody thought we'd all be blown up but of course nothing happened. Then we began to notice food shortages and that sort of thing. My most abiding memories include the day they dropped 'the big bomb' and the night they dropped the 'stick of five' bombs across the houses down by Blackstones.

Michael Tebbutt

Mangolds

I was a child in the First World War. I remember one winter evening standing with my father at the front window of our house in Doughty Street. There were flashes of bombs which were being dropped at Clipsham. I was told it was because a field of mangolds had been pulled and heaped into a pile. Then it snowed and a German Zeppelin pilot thought they were tents because the moonlight was shining on them. Another night a bomb dropped just the other side of Blackstone's works. There was a great explosion and all the lights at Blackstone's went out. It cracked some of the ceilings there but as it fell in the water there wasn't much damage.

Dick Grimwood

Welcome Harum-Scarums!

Opposite Walker's Bookshop there used to be a pub called The Pineapple (now Woolworths) which was frequented by the Americans and the Poles. All the American officers were in the George and all the harum-scarums were around the town.

Eunice Sorfleet

Blackout

We were on standby the whole time and our main duty was guarding certain points. There was always a guard at the railway stations and there was a guard on the bridge over the railway station.

We had to cover the windows at the back of the shop with black paper which had to be put up in the evening and taken down in the morning. The blinds had to be light-proof and we had to put sticky tape on the windows in case of blasts which could shatter the glass. There was an enormous amount of work and it was very difficult. In those days we stayed open until six normally, but on Fridays, market day, we stayed open until seven and on Saturdays we stayed open until the cinema closed! We opened at nine but my father was an early riser and he was always there before I was. I remember coming out of the shop one evening in the blackout and walking straight into somebody. I think we must have hit nose to nose! I never saw them and I never knew who it was.

Stuart Rodgers

Daren't Show a Light

We were living in St George's Street and our house had sliding windows. My father made frames to fit them and fixed blackout material to it. At night we'd go around the house and push them into the windows and then draw the curtains. You had to be ever so careful because you daren't show a light. I was a Warden and had to wear an armband and be on duty in the street.

Maggie Graham

Called Out!

I'd been out one day on my bicycle and I came back to find my mother and father waiting for me. They said I was called out so I grabbed my rifle and hat and my armband and rushed up to the school which was the assembly point. There had been a report of parachutists coming down so various people were sent out to look for them. I was the youngest there and unfortunately the captain put me in charge of the ammunition. They didn't find any parachutists so I didn't miss much!

Stuart Rodgers

Wet Feet

My father built an air-raid shelter in the garden. He dug a trench and put corrugated iron over the top and made a temporary door he propped up against it. But if it rained, you couldn't get in because it was full of water! We'd go down the meadows catching

Margaret (Maggie) Graham (*née* Clark).

minnows and we'd put them in there! If there was a daytime raid we had to go in there so my brother and I would sit with our feet up when it was wet. We had an Anderson shelter which was for indoors. It was as big as a double bed and there was like a cage on the side. Mum had to move out all her furniture to get it in the room. We had to get in there at night if there was a raid although we spent some time behind the piano which Mum said was the strongest piece of furniture we had.

Eunice Sorfleet

New Homes

When I first lived in Lincoln Road they built fifty houses for the soldiers coming home. Talk about fights! Everybody was marching down to the council offices. 'Why had she got one and we haven't got one?' I got one because I'd got two children and lived with my mother-in-law. Clark and Belton's built ours. Rick's built some and Bowman's built some. They were all local builders. I got the key one Friday lunchtime and I went straight there – and never went back to my mother-in-law! When I look back, she was a kind old soul to take us in.

Freda Clark

Sweets

Richard, my brother, and I always had some sweets on a Saturday night. Usually it was a small bar of chocolate or something like that. Sweets were rationed in wartime.

Pamela Clark

Shattered

They dropped a bomb which shattered a lot of the windows in Burghley House.

Eunice Sorfleet

150 Yards Away

It was 150 yards from the north-west corner of the house and the crater persisted for many years.

E.C. Till

Sidney Allen (far right back row) with colleagues in the Auxiliary Fire Service (AFS) during the Second World War.

Fresh Vegetables

My father, Sidney Allen, apart from being first in the AFS, often used to work overtime at Martin's Cultivator Works and he always had an allotment. He'd go straight there from work to his garden which was down the Uffington Road. He grew loads of potatoes and greens and we always had fresh vegetables. Men always got a bit extra.

Doris Borowik

Poles Apart

The Poles were at Easton and the Americans at Walcot Hall.

Eunice Sorfleet

There were many people who were billeted in Stamford. In particular we had the Polish airborne contingent here. They were a very friendly, jolly crowd.

Michael Tebbutt

The British Restaurant

The British Restaurant was in Cheyne Lane. All towns had one. Ours was where the Chinese Restaurant is. During the war you could go there and have a cheap meal. And they were good, too. You didn't have to take your ration book or use coupons.

Eunice Sorfleet

Cat Food

The corner shop at the end of Alexandra Road used to be a grocer's shop and when the Italians were here used to buy cat food and go back to the brick works where they worked and heat them up in the kiln. That was their meal.

Grahamme Sorfleet

Clothing Coupons

We had coupons for clothes and food and furniture. My first suite came on coupons. I didn't have enough for a settee but I had enough for two armchairs. I got some curtain material on dockets.

Maggie Graham

Maggie Graham's National Identity Card.

A wedding day photograph of Maggie (Margaret) Clarke and Sidney Graham

Sewing and Knitting

We had lots of laughs and being the age we were we didn't take the war as seriously as our parents. My mum used to go with a lot of other ladies and make shirts for the soldiers. They used to knit boot stocking out of oily wool. They went down to the town hall where they sat and sewed and knitted.

Eunice Sorfleet

The Icing on the Cake

Mr Marshall baked my wedding cake but he wasn't allowed to almond paste it or ice it. He brought the cake down to us and he brought some icing sugar and some almond paste and told me I could do it myself. There was Mrs Footitt who used to have a dairy and I asked her if she could come and help me. We managed to get the almond paste on and all the icing. Then I went around all the family and collected all the little bits and bobs that they'd had on their wedding cakes and we put them all over the cake! When I sent some away to relatives, my sister gave me her top tier of her wedding cake that she'd had by her and I cut that up and sent that too! She was married eighteen months before me.

Maggie Graham

Corned Beef

You had to have corned beef to make your ration up. And we had powdered eggs and if there was any bananas or things like that, they had to go to people with children first.

You had to queue to try and buy oranges.

Maggie Graham

Coupons

During the war we were lucky as we only had one bomb drop. We had blackout curtains and the light was dimmed. Sweets were rationed and I think you could have four ounces a week. We had to count the sweet coupons carefully because they were more important than money then.

Alice Burton

Eating Snails

On Empingham Road there was a prisoner-of-war camp. They were allowed to walk around the town but they had big yellow disks on the back of their uniforms. They worked on the land. Some went to Burghley and some to the wood yard. They were all over the town. A lot of the Italian prisoners-of-war worked at the gas works. They used to go along the river bank and collect snails – and they ate them!

Eunice Sorfleet

Petrol Rationing

Ray, Vic Davis and I were in the Forces during the war so Ruby, my sister had to take over Vic's bread round. Petrol was rationed and was very difficult to come by. Bread was also rationed and counting the bread coupons and filling in the appropriate forms was no light task. Travelling in the van when it was dark was quite dangerous as the headlights had to be partially blacked out until only a slit remained.

Keeping the business going during the war was difficult for my father so he applied to the Army for leave of absence for me. I was given three months' compassionate leave to help in the bakehouse. It was hard work! I was glad to go back!

Terence Asker

Trampled Garden

We lived in the police houses in Cliffe Road. One night there was an air raid and they dropped incendiary bombs. Mum was convinced that they'd dropped one in our garden. Now my father had got carrots, beetroot and all sorts of vegetables, so she rang the police station to say there was a bomb in the garden. All these air raid wardens and policemen came and searched the garden but couldn't find anything. The next morning my father looked out of the window and found they had tramped over everything!

Eunice Sorfleet

Bells

One night the church bells sounded. They always said that if England was invaded the bells would be rung. My mother said I'm going down to see

123

that my door's locked. I'm not having any Germans coming here and taking our food!

Maggie Graham

A Football Stadium

We played cricket on Empingham Road where the German prisoner-of-war camp was. They were good footballers and they built their own football stadium. They built a bank all the way round so that you could stand on the bank and see everything. When the camp was closed, they levelled it all off and it became the Empingham Road Playing Fields.

Grahamme Sorfleet

Joan Wilcox, later Shaw, in 1946.

Stamford's Gratitude

My husband, Leslie Burton, was in the Fleet Air Arm. When he came out of the forces he was given a cigarette box which has the Stamford Crest on it and the words 'A token of Stamford's gratitude 1939-1945' and his name, Petty Officer W.L. Burton. It was presented to him and everyone who had served in the war had one.

Alice Burton

Workshop

My father owned half an acre of land in Brownlow Gardens and he grew vegetables. At the end of the rows he used to plant asters. We always had fresh vegetables and I used to sell them in the shop at times. My father had a wall fall down and the money it was going to cost to build it up again was rather a lot so instead of doing that he built a row of garages. There were twelve and he let them for a shilling a night. During the war the Polish Parachute Regiment were here and they had one as a workshop for repairing ambulances. They used to come and visit us and we used to play cards with them.

Alice Burton

Hospital

My husband was stationed at number 31 St Paul's Street. At the back they had Nissen huts and my husband worked in the hospital there.

Then they were moved to the bottom of King's Mill Lane.

Doris Borowik

Whistle Blower

I used to go to dances at the Lansbury Hall. All the girls did. The pilots used to come from Wittering in their flying jackets and their flying boots. They used to walk in and we'd think, ooh, lovely, all these men! Then the flight sergeant would fling open the door, blow a whistle – and they'd all gone! There was an Australian bomber crew who used to come as well and the pilot, well, all the girls thought he was wonderful! Tall, blond and they wore navy uniforms. The Free French were at Wittering and we used to see them.

Eunice Sorfleet

Dancing

There used to be a dance every night at the Lansbury Hall and one at Blackstone's on a Friday. That finished at eleven o'clock because I think they need the canteen for the works. At the Lansbury it was about an hour later. We used to do quicksteps, foxtrots, tangos, the Hokey-Cokey, the Lambeth Walk and the Palais Glide. I was very fond of the old-fashioned waltz – the Viennese Waltz. And of course, with so many Poles, we had to have a polka! At the end they'd play 'Who's taking you home tonight?' or 'Goodnight Sweetheart'.

Doris Borowik

The Forces Club

My mum used to go down and look after the Forces' Club which was in what is now the Arts Centre Theatre. They had all kinds of games – snooker and that sort of thing.

Eunice Sorfleet

Tanks in the Ballroom?

I can remember when there were tanks in the ballroom at the Arts Centre! They were Bren gun carriers and they got two in there.

Grahamme Sorfleet

Eyes Right!

In the war, I was in the Girls' Training Corps and I used to go regularly. Miss Garnetto was one of the leaders and her father kept one of the cinemas. We learnt Morse code and map reading but mainly we seemed to be marching about. We always went on a parade to one of the churches once a month. Once we were coming down Star Lane and a group of Poles were marching towards us on the way to the Catholic church and as they came round the corner, whoever was in charge of them said 'Eyes right.' We couldn't stop laughing!

Doris Borowik

The Girls' Training Corps on parade in Broad Street on Empire Youth Sunday, 21 May 1945.

"HOME GUARD"

Martin's Section.

Standing Orders.

28-8-40.

No.1. In the event of an Air Raid by day. the Duty Patrol including H.Q. will at once proceed home for their Uniforms, Rifles & Respirators and report back at the Works for duty. After the"All Clear" Rifles & Uniforms will be taken to the Fire Station, and locked up for the day.

No.2. In the event of an Air Raid at night, Patrols will carry on as usual and in future there must be no smoking on duty, striking of matches or showing any lights is strictly forbidden. When a sentry is posted no man are allowed to congregate in front of the Works Gates by night. They must patrol or remain at C.H.Q. Patrols must carry their ammunitions in their tunic pocket, and Rifles must not be be loaded or fired without orders from their Patrol Leader. Only Ten Rounds of ammunition per man are to be carried.

No.3. In the event of a General Alarm all men would at once proceed home for their Uniforms and Rifles etc., and man their respective posts and await further instructions.

No.4. Apart from "A.R.P." personell and "Home Guard" no one would be allowed inside the Works buildings during an Air Raid by day.

No.5. During an Air Raid by Night the Works property would be closed completely to any public person, apart from"Home Guard". and "A.R.P." personell.

(Signed) *S.H.R.Allen. Sgt.*

...S..H..R..Allen... Section Commander.

Home Guard Standing Orders, 1940.

Food Parcels

We used to have powdered egg and powdered milk and one of the Americans we knew told his mother about us and she used to send me parcels. There used to be dehydrated mincemeat, aprons, handkerchiefs, nylons.

Eunice Sorfleet

Home Guard

My father, Sidney Allen, formed the Home Guard at Martin's Cultivator Works in Ryhall Road. At the beginning of the war he was in the Auxiliary Fire Service and he left that when he was asked to form the Home Guard.

Doris Borowik

Our Turn for Offal?

We were registered with Mr Hazel, the butcher who was in Red Lion Street, where the delicatessen is. You took your turn for the offal and your name would eventually come up. Not everyone wanted it. Mother always used to stuff sheep's heart and bake it. We were registered for other things with Bowman & Essex at the bottom of Ironmonger Street. It was Miss Bowman and Mr Essex and they were grocers. We used to have dried egg and we'd try to make it into scrambled egg but it was very peculiar. Mother used to cook tripe and onions in the evening to fill us up.

Doris Borowik

Canteen

There was a canteen in St Mary's Street where the theatre is now and I used to go there to help.

Margie Harvey

Pony and Cart

We had the bakery and you couldn't get petrol so my father had to invest in a pony and cart to do his deliveries. He delivered to most of Stamford and to Casterton, Uffington and to some of the outlying farms. When things got easier and he started delivering by van again he went to places like Wilsthorpe and the Bourne area.

Harold Harvey

Evacuees

The White House, which is at the top of St Martin's next to the Garden House Hotel, was a place for evacuees who had things like impetigo and eczema. They were there with a matron and one qualified nurse. During the war I used to help there as an auxiliary.

Margie Harvey

Sam Brown Belts

In the last few months of the war American soldiers were stationed in Stamford. They paraded every morning outside the police station dressed in grey shirts and trousers and boots. They had Sam Brown belts and Stetson hats.

Dick Grimwood

Useful

There was the Drill Hall, the Oddfellows' Hall, the Lansbury Hall and the Assembly Rooms which were all very useful during the war. The Albert Hall was where Tesco's is and was pulled down in the Sixties. You went through a house where there were meeting rooms and then through the garden to a hall at the back. It was not very grand.

Mark Hooson

Hops

When the war was on there were Saturday Night Hops at the Assembly Rooms for local people. Upstairs were the cloakrooms.

Harold Harvey

A Tank

They once brought a tank to display on St Mary's Hill during the first war. We had a Service of Thanksgiving after the Armistice was declared and this was held outside Brown's Hospital. Large numbers went to it.

Margaret Hare

VE Day

I don't think we celebrated VE Day here very much. I think there was a parade and the children had tea parties but I can't remember anything particular.

Dick Grimwood